ON HISTORY

By the same author

Experience and its Modes

A Guide to the Classics (with G. T. Griffith)

Social and Political Doctrines of Contemporary Europe

Hobbes's Leviathan

The Voice of Poetry in the Conversation of Mankind

Rationalism in Politics and Other Essays

Hobbes on Civil Association

On Human Conduct

ON HISTORY
AND OTHER ESSAYS

Michael Oakeshott

Barnes and Noble Books
Totowa · New Jersey

© Michael Oakeshott 1983

First published in the USA 1983 by
Barnes and Noble Books
81 Adams Drive, Totowa, New Jersey 07512

Library of Congress Cataloging in Publication Data

Oakeshott, Michael Joseph, 1901–
    On history and other essays.

    Includes index.
        1. Historiography—Addresses, essays, lectures.
        2. Interpersonal relations—Addresses, essays, lectures.
        3. Babel, Tower of—Addresses, essays, lectures.
    I. Title.
    D13.0'23   1983   907'.2   82–22617
    ISBN 0-389-20355-6

Printed in Great Britain

Contents

To all who, over the years, have been members of the seminar on the history of political thought in the London School of Economics

Three Essays on History

I Present, Future and Past

1

The word 'history' is ambiguous; it is commonly used in at least two different senses. In one it stands for the notional grand total of all that has ever happened in the lives of human beings, or for a passage of somehow related occurrences distinguished in this grand total by being specified in terms of a place and a time and a substantive identity. This meaning appears in such expressions as 'the history of the world', 'the history of the Jews', 'the history of Switzerland', or 'the early history of the Bank of England'. Here the adjective 'historical' means what actually happened there and then, in respect of this identity, whether or not we know anything whatever about it. And the 'makers' of such 'history' are the participants in the occurrences.

In another meaning, 'history' stands for a certain sort of enquiry into, and a certain sort of understanding of, some such passage of occurrences; the engagement and the conclusions of an historian. And this meaning appears in such expressions as 'an historical dictionary of the English language', or 'when reading Ranke or Maitland one feels oneself to be in the presence of a remarkable historical imagination', or 'A history of England'. Here the adjective 'historical' denotes an enquiry which, whatever we may think about the truth or reliability of its conclusions, is recognized in terms of certain characteristics to be an historical enquiry and not one of another sort; and it denotes the kind of understanding reached in the course of such an enquiry. And here 'history' is recognized to be 'made' not by those whose words or deeds are investigated but by an historian.

These two meanings are distinct but they are not discrepant. They are brought and held together in an expression such as *Mommsen's Römische Geschichte*, which means (or purports to mean) an understanding of occurrences set down by Mommsen as the result of a certain sort of enquiry, namely, the enquiry that distinguishes an historian. Mommsen had no hand in making the Roman Republic, but he may be said to be one of the makers of the history of the Roman Republic.

I am concerned here with 'history' in the second of these senses; with history as an enquiry and with the character of an historical enquiry. I shall take the word 'history' to mean a distinguishable mode of enquiry, and the expression 'historical understanding' to identify a distinct mode of understanding. And by the modality of an enquiry I mean the conditions of relevance that constitute it a distinct kind of enquiry and distinguish it both from an inconsequential groping around in the confusion of all that may be going on and from similarly distinct enquiries but of other kinds. These conditions of relevance are of course formal, but where there are none, where there is no specifiable modality, there can be no enquiry and so no consequential conclusions.

A mode of understanding, then, is not merely an attitude or a point of view. It is an autonomous manner of understanding, specifiable in terms of exact conditions, which is logically incapable of denying or confirming the conclusions of any other mode of understanding, or indeed of making any relevant utterance in respect of it. And what I am looking for are the conditions of relevance in terms of which an enquiry may be recognized as an 'historical' enquiry.

There are two common objections to this project which may be noticed at this point because they are both warnings against even undertaking it. First, it is said that historical enquiry is a human invention; that it is to be found nowhere save in the writings of alleged historians; that these, so far from displaying a uniform character, exhibit a great variety of diverse engagements; and that there is no discernible trend in the changing styles of historical enquiry that might lead us to suppose them to be stages on the way to some definitive condition or to be insignificant circumstantial deviations from such a condition. Or, as one writer suggests, historical enquiry is not a distinct 'mode of thought' but should be regarded as 'the common home of many interests and techniques and traditions devised by those who have dedicated their best energies to the study of the past'.

Now, beyond question historical enquiry is the invention of historians and it is proper that they should defend the inventiveness with which they have pursued it from what they suspect are the tiresome attentions of a philosophical Procrustes. But it does not follow that no distinctive logical character is attributable to historical understanding, and the suspicion is misplaced. The variety and changefulness of the enquiries and the conclusions of the physical sciences certainly do not make it a lost endeavour to seek a logic of scientific understanding. And this identification of historical enquiry as a variety of undertakings joined in being concerned with the past itself recognizes it to have at least some distinctive character capable of further specification. What does an exclusive concern with the past entail? And further, historians have nothing to fear for their freedom of movement within the home composed of their various interests and techniques from an attempt to explore history as a mode of understanding. The conditions which may constitute it a mode of understanding are not formulae for conducting an historical enquiry or premeditated norms to which it should subscribe; they are its theoretical postulates and they are reflected in a piece of historical writing only as presuppositions which specify it as an enquiry of a certain sort and distinguish it from other sorts of enquiry.

The second objection runs somewhat as follows: historical enquiry is concerned with understanding, or, as they say (I think mistakenly), 'explanation'. And, since (it is alleged) there cannot be categorially incommensurable modes of understanding, an engagement to specify a distinctively historical mode of understanding can be no more than a misconceived attempt to discern in historical enquiry the principles common to all valid understanding. Further, it is claimed that the model of all valid understanding is that of 'scientific' explanation; that is, explanation in terms of 'general laws' or regularities relating to what are recognized as components of a 'process'. Consequently, the proper occupation of anyone concerned with the character of historical understanding is not to seek an impossible distinctiveness but to exhibit it in terms of this exemplar. This view of the matter no doubt merits careful consideration; it cannot, I think, be sustained, but neither can it be abruptly dismissed. Nevertheless, instead of considering it now, and rather than allowing it to deter me from my project, I shall come back to it in my second essay where it relates to what I have to say about historical events and their relations to one another.

Three further preliminary considerations may be noticed. First, my concern here is not with what may be called the methodology of historical enquiry. It may be that there are certain methods of investigation appropriate, or even peculiar, to historical enquiry. Indeed attempts have been made to formulate such methods and to present them either prescriptively or as criteria for assessing the substantive conclusions of an historical enquiry. But whatever may be the status of such methods, they are not what I mean by the conditions or postulates which distinguish history as a mode of understanding.

Secondly, I am not concerned with what is sometimes called the 'sociology' of historical enquiry; that is, the consideration of an alleged piece of historical writing in respect of the manner in which it reflects the current circumstances of an historian, his affections, his prejudices, his allegiances, his perception of current needs and whatever 'concerns' or ulterior purposes he may have for choosing his particular engagement. Why, for example, did Gibbon abandon his project of writing a history of Switzerland and turn to the decline and fall of the Roman Empire, or what attracted Mommsen's attention to Imperial Rome or Ranke's to seventeenth-century England? What structure of contemporary circumstances may be called upon to account for the efflorescence of historical enquiry concerned with both English 'constitutional' and 'economic' history in the late nineteenth century, or the current concern in the United States of America with the history of 'slavery', ancient and modern? Considerations of this sort, which are to do with an historian's choice of engagement, and which may blinker his enquiry, suggest hitherto unexplored lines of investigation, or otherwise condition the course it takes, lie to one side of my concern. Whatever significance they may have as indicators of an historian's range of imagination, they cannot be adduced to support or to qualify the contention that his is, indeed, an historical enquiry and not one of another sort. Nor am I concerned with the 'history' of historical enquiry; that is, with discerning and trying historically to account for changes in historiographical design or practice. I am concerned with what may, perhaps, be called the logic of historical enquiry, 'logic' being understood as a concern not with the truth of conclusions but with the conditions in terms of which they may be recognized to be conclusions.

Thirdly, a mode of understanding cannot be specified in terms of a so-called subject matter; here, as always, the conditions of understanding specify what is to be understood. This is not because some things have histories and others do not, but because to have a history is to have been endowed with it in being understood in a certain manner.

And my concern is to specify the conditions of a mode of understanding which endows whatever is to be understood with historicity.

Now, the word 'history' denotes an engagement of enquiry which has emerged without premonition from the indiscriminate gropings of human intelligence and has come to acquire recognizable shape. Like other such engagements, its shape is somewhat indistinct. Its practitioners are notoriously generous; they have been apt to keep open house to all who have seemingly similar concerns, to welcome and to accommodate a miscellany of intellectual enterprises and to find virtue in their variety. Nevertheless, taken at this level, and even when it is recognized merely in terms of the directions of enquiry followed by writers commonly alleged to be historians, it is not an entirely indiscriminate engagement. It has some identifying marks, some characteristic organizing ideas and a vocabulary of expressions to which it has given specialized meanings: 'past', 'happening', 'situation', 'event', 'cause', 'change' and so on. As they come to us, these marks of identity are often obscure and ambiguous. Nevertheless, to recognize them is to make our first groping attempt to distinguish and take hold of a current manner of enquiry, and it is with them that the enterprise of eliciting the logic of historical understanding must begin. This is a theoretical undertaking designed, not only to assemble a distinct, coherent, ideal mode of understanding in terms of its necessary conditions, but also to sustain the contention that it may properly be recognized as an 'historical' mode of understanding by relating these necessary conditions to the identifying marks which give to this current and contingent manner of enquiry its somewhat indistinct shape. And it is with these that we may make our start.

Accordingly, I propose to begin by identifying history as a mode of enquiry and understanding in terms of an idea of past, an idea of an event and of some significant relationship to be established between events, and an idea of change. It is not suggested that this is an exhaustive list of the terms of historical understanding; there are others which will emerge in considering these. Nor is it alleged that, as they stand and without further specification, they combine to constitute a distinct 'historical' mode of under-standing, or indeed any categorially distinct mode of understanding; *that* may appear (if it appears at all) only in a further determination of these expressions. Thus, I pro-pose to make manageable the question, What is the character of historical enquiry and understanding? by resolving it into the questions, What precise and distinctive meaning may be attributed to the expressions 'historical past', 'historical change', 'historical event' and 'historical relationship between events'? And although I must con-sider these questions *seriatim*, none can be fully answered until they are all answered. I shall begin with the notion 'historical past'.

2

We are concerned with our awareness of past and, within it, the character of a distinguishable 'historical' awareness of past.

The world upon which I open my eyes is unmistakably present. If I stand at the street corner and describe to myself what I perceive I speak to myself in the present tense. But even for me, a relatively unconcerned spectator, this present may be (and usually is) qualified by an awareness of future or of past or of both future and past.

A man is standing on the kerb, and if this is all I perceive then present is not significantly qualified. Of course, what I perceive is a going-on; time passes. But what I am attending to is a continuous present in which the passage of time is marked by no noticeable change or even suggestion of movement. On the other hand, if what I perceive is a man standing on the kerb and waiting to cross the street or to keep an assignation, then present is qualified by an awareness of future. And this awareness of future is not evoked by neglecting present or pushing it on one side, but by attending to it exactly. I have nothing to go upon but present perception and the recollected experience with which it is informed, and future is evoked in the way he is standing, perhaps the movement of his eyes, in the perception of endeavour or expectancy. The situation is one of incipient movement: a future infinitive. And the fact that on this occasion I may be mistaken is, of course, irrelevant. Future, then, is an understanding of present in terms of a change it may be perceived to intimate.

I turn my attention elsewhere and perceive a man with a wooden leg hobbling by; and if this is all I perceive, present is not significantly qualified. Certainly the man moves, he passes me by, and there is future to attend to if I am disposed to attend to it. Where is he going? But in respect of his having a wooden leg he is a continuous present. On the other hand, if what I perceive is a man who has lost one of his legs and has acquired a wooden one in its place, then present has been qualified by past. And this awareness of past is evoked, not by neglecting present, but in a reading of present which evokes past expressed in the word 'lost'. Past, then, is an understanding of present in terms of a change it may be perceived to record or to conserve.

No doubt, there are some goings-on which, while being recognized as present, tend to evoke future rather than past: a railway timetable which we read in terms of what it tells we may expect. And there are others which tend to evoke past: an out-of-date railway timetable. But there is no present incapable of evoking either future or past if we read it in a manner to do so. Both future and past, then, emerge only in a reading of present; and a particular future or past is one eligible to be evoked from a particular present and is contingently related to the particular present from which it may be evoked: the waiting man doing what he is waiting to do, and the bygone occurrence in which the one-legged man suffered his loss.

I am concerned here with present and past and with the

contention that the expression 'historical past' denotes a distinguishable mode of past. Consequently, what falls to be considered are the conditions in terms of which any mode of past may be distinguished and (within these conditions) those which may define an historical past. And I shall argue that a mode of past is to be distinguished in terms of the modal conditions of the present to which it is related, and that among those conditions is a proper procedure in which it may be evoked.

We begin in a present, and here in a present related to past. It is composed of objects (Winchester Cathedral, a letter I have received, a performance I am witnessing) each of which is recognized to have a past of its own composed of antecedents related to it, and to be the starting-place from which that past may be evoked. Such a present determines what particular past shall be sought, and the relationship between this present and its past is contingent. But each such present object or happening is identified not only as something in particular perceived, but also in terms of its modal character. For example, it may be recognized in terms of its current usefulness or perhaps in terms of its aesthetic qualities. As objects of attention and concern they must be recognized (at least tacitly) in some modal terms; no object is unconditionally recognizable. And in this respect the past to which they are related will be a past constituted in terms of modal conditions which match those of this present. This relationship between present and past is a necessary relationship: present and past here are logical counterparts. Thus an enquiry concerned to distinguish the conditions of an alleged 'historical' mode of past must begin by considering the modalities of present. And its design is to specify a modally distinct present to which a past, at once itself modally distinct and having some claim to be called 'historical', is necessarily related and from which it may be evoked. But further, a necessary component of a present in respect of its relationship to past is a procedure in which past may be evoked from it. It may, for example, be a procedure of critical

enquiry or perhaps merely of recollection. And this procedure belongs to the modal conditions of a present. It
specifies, not what particular contingent past occurrences
may be recognized as its antecedents, but the modal
conditions of that past. Consequently, a modally distinct
'historical' past is identifiable in terms of the procedure
required to evoke it from a modally distinct present.

In short, my enquiry to discern the conditions of a
modally distinct 'historical' past will assume historical
understanding to be an engagement exclusively concerned
with past and will seek a modally distinct present which
supplies both the conditions from which such an engagement may take off and the procedure in which it may be
pursued.

But before embarking upon it I shall pause to consider a
contention which, if it could be sustained, would go far to
nullifying my proposed undertaking. This contention is
that there is a present, usually called the practical present,
which exhibits (among much else) an awareness of past, a
concern with past, a disposition to evoke past and is
equipped with a procedure in which to do so; that this
present is unconditional, emancipated from modality,
'primordial' and inescapable; and that, consequently, the
past which corresponds to it is similarly unconditional and
inescapable, the only genuine past. Thus to seek another
and different so-called 'historical' past is a lost endeavour. I
shall consider first the character of this present and that of
the past which corresponds to it, and then the claims made
on their behalf.

3

An ordinary sort of human life, such as we all must lead, is
inhabiting and responding to a present composed of
objects and happenings, distinguished in all that may be
going on, distinct from one another, and related to
ourselves as the objects of our attention and concern. On

any occasion this attention will have a focus, and this present will include objects which are not, on this occasion, raised to the status of objects of concern. As I search a shop window for a pair of shoes to satisfy my wants I may be aware of the sheet of glass before me and the pavement under my feet, but they are not objects of concern, although of course they may become so. Objects of attention and concern are recognized as examples of some handy universal (or ideal character) and are recognized in terms of their qualities and of the expectations they evoke; that is, they are understood in relation to ourselves as agents. Our responses to them (that which constitutes them 'objects') are appreciations of their current meaning and worth to ourselves in respect of their qualities.

Each of us occupies such a present as his own; it is a personal present. But it is not composed of so-called 'primordial subjective experiences' and our relation to it is not 'immediate' or 'intuitive' as distinct from reflective. My Venice is not your Venice, and this grove of trees, which to me now is a shelter from the rain or a place to play hide-and-seek, to another (or to me in different circumstances) may be a defence against soil erosion. But there is nothing subjective or esoteric about these various understandings. They may exclude one another but they do not deny one another, and they may be recognized by those who do not share them. Every such object is the perception of a subject, but none is 'subjective' in the sense of being outside discourse or impervious to error. 'Subjectivity' is not an ontological category.

This, then, is a present of common discourse and we come to inhabit it by learning to do so. Learning here is learning to notice, to distinguish and to identify these objects in terms of their qualities: their shapes, features, characteristics, properties, propensities, likenesses and unlikenesses, habitats and their connections with one another. It is learning to recognize their meanings and worth in relation to our purposes, our wants and to the actions and utterances in which we seek to satisfy those wants. It is learning where they are to be found (or where they are 'kept'), how to assemble and to enjoy them, how to understand them and perhaps how to use them to make artefacts which are themselves objects fabricated and known in terms of their qualities. Mistakes may be made which lead to disappointments; what one learns another may remain ignorant of; capacities for learning may differ; some skills are more difficult than others to acquire. And there is said to be a pathological condition, called *apraxia*, in which a subject is still able to identify an object (such as a horse) or an artefact (a knife or a spade) as a concretion of qualities, but has lost all sense of the purpose for which it might be used or for which it was designed and is, thus, incapable of recognizing it as an object of practical concern, and yet does not replace it in his perception with an object of any other sort – an object of worship, of love or of poetic contemplation.

The objects which compose this present are not, then, the mere furnishings of an abode in which our doings take place; they are themselves the abode. They are themselves the language in which we compose our wants and conduct the transactions designed to satisfy them, the terms of our habits, the steps of our wanderings to and fro. Every such object noticed and attended to is a distinct happening recognized in relation to ourselves as agents, responded to, valued, used, put by, ignored or rejected. Self as agent and object as concretion of qualities are counterparts of one another, distinguishable but inseparable. There may, of course, be moments of half-release when we walk for the pleasure of it and jump for joy (not to clear a hedge), when a tree is a marvel, the moon a mystery, the sea a miracle, a wheatfield holy, a fish sacred, and the sound of the flute in the market place a reconciliation; but these are objects of another kind. Among the constituents of this universe of practical discourse are other persons related to ourselves in terms of usefulness and convenience but also in terms of moral (that is, non-instrumental) considerations and compunctions, but not in the poetic terms of affection, friendship and love which belong to another world.

These objects of our concern are recognized to be distributed in space: that is, they are recognized in terms, not of a concept of space, but in respect of their positions relative to ourselves, to our wants and to one another. They are 'here', 'close by' or 'over there'; 'near', 'to hand', 'far away' or 'out of reach'. And their worth to us (that is, our understanding of them as objects of practical concern) is, in part, a function of their positions in relation to ourselves: a bird in the hand is worth two in the bush, and the remoteness of the Andaman Islands recommends them to one who has enemies in London whom he wishes to escape. And even when these distances (and amounts) are expressed in measurements, they refer to conveniences (not to mere 'facts') and are related to our wants and satisfactions. A distance may be 'the time it takes'. Position relative to ourselves is one of the qualities of such objects.

Perhaps more significantly, we recognize these objects in terms of time; not a concept of time, but of 'now' and 'then', of 'soon' and 'later' and of 'the time it takes' expressed in some conventional manner. In the first place, this is a recognition of objects in terms of their qualities of change-fulness, eligibility to be changed and their durability. Here, time is a relation between a present and an imagined future condition of things relative to ourselves. Thus, the present we occupy in practical understanding evokes future. Indeed, it evokes a variety of futures: a conjectural future, a future foreseen, one which (in addition) evokes fear or in which we have invested our hopes, an intended and sought-for future etc., but always a future related to and of the same kind as this present. With every want we evoke a future, and in every action we seek a future condition of things, uncertain of achievement and sure only of its transience. In short, this present of practical engagement is not merely intermittently related to future; it is itself a present-future. The objects which compose it, in being recognized in terms of their worth to us in relation to our practical engagements, are recognized in terms of the future they foretell or of their eligibility to satisfy our wants. In this universe of discourse we live always in a future, near or more distant.[1]

The present–future of practical understanding is also related to past. And past here is, of course, a past related to this present; that is, our practical concern with past is our concern with present objects in relation to ourselves, to ascertain their worth to us and to use them for the satisfaction of our wants. But here I must descend into detail because this past is not only (like the practical future) various but it concerns us particularly on account of our concern here with an alleged 'historical past'.

First, each of us as an agent concerned with a present–future is related to the past which this present encapsulates: a past composed of all that has happened to us (often without our being aware of it at the time), of all that we have suffered, done, imagined, thought, believed (and perhaps long since ceased to believe), and known to us in the residue it has left behind. A component of this residue (our present) may sometimes be a recognizable mark the past has left upon us, or this residue may be what we now are in some more general respect. I need hardly specify. The scarcely attended to happenings and doings which have now turned into habits, the long unrecorded hours of 'practice' which went to make the current skill of a pianist, the forgotten encounters in books or in conversation which

[1] To some who have considered it, this inconclusive, episodic character of human conduct has seemed to convict it of 'absurdity' and this devotion of ourselves to the transitory objects of our concern in terms of an ever-receding future has been deplored as a regrettable 'dissipation' or a deplorable indignity. And it is said that this would be remedied if these engagements to procure the evanescent satisfaction of transitory wants were transformed by being understood as steps in the performance of some 'central task' or in the unfolding of a 'destiny' other than death. With this, however, we are not now concerned.

contributed to what now exists as an intellectual character, the bygone experiences which now appear as a (perhaps regretted) suspicious disposition, the hardly noticed accident in childhood which is now a scar, and I do not know what else. Bits of this past are said to 'catch up on us': the unconsidered nights spent standing sentry in the rain which thirty years later appear as a rheumatic shoulder; a long-forgotten promise which comes home to roost in a belated demand that it be fulfilled. And since we are concerned with what happened in respect of its reflection in what we are, we should perhaps include our genetic past: the organization of genes which distinguished that unknown great-grandfather which now appears in the colour of my eyes and the shape (and, in part, the skill) of my hands. What comes after may modify what went before, but it cannot expunge it. Layer upon layer; all a great and contingent mixture from which we cannot escape but to which what we are and what we do now is somehow a response. And I call this an encapsulated past because its relation to us now does not in any way depend upon its being recollected. Much of it is beyond recall, and whatever significance it may have is nothing at all to do with its being recalled. It is what Pascal called *la raison des effets* untouched by *la pensée de derrière*.

Secondly, there is a remembered past. By taking thought we may, perhaps, distinguish a remembered past within a present state of consciousness, but every such state is a manifold in which present and a remembered past are inextricably joined. What memory supplies is not an itemized past but a continuity of consciousness in which I recognize myself as a continuing identity and my present experiences and engagements as my own. Memory may sometimes be self-justification but the awareness of past in memory is always self-awareness.

Thirdly, there is a recollected or a consulted past. This is a reputedly already known past of itemized experiences recalled to mind for whatever it may contain of guidance or use for the successful pursuit of our current practical engagements. Our access to it is in a procedure, not of research, but of recall: we may recall only what is already familiar to us and we do recall only what may be believed to be appropriate to our current circumstances and engagements. Like the remembered past, it is a personal but not, of course, a 'subjective' past.

Some part of this recollected past is composed of our own earlier experiences of living in the world, as distinct from the habits, the practices and the skills we may have learned and which are available without any reflective engagement in recollection. What is recalled may be no more than a useful piece of information or a somewhat vague reminiscence which bids us take care, or it may be a situation allegedly similar to that which is now engaging our attention and which we recall for the advice it may have to offer. But whatever is recalled, recollection here is joining a puzzling or intractable present with a known and unproblematic past to compose a less puzzling or more manageable practical present. Here, there is something like genuine *pensée de derrière*, although it is not the pastness of the recalled experiences (and certainly not their actual situation in our past experience) which is significant but their familiarity and their relevance to present circumstances.

But besides our own recalled past experiences (and, of course, those of other living persons whom we may consult) our practical present contains an ever-increasing deposit of what are reputed to be fragments of a past which have survived, not as a wound survives in a scar but on account of their never having perished, which are now available to be listened to and consulted and which may be related to our current conduct. They may be artefacts (perhaps recognized as models to be copied), recorded anecdotes or episodes of bygone human fortune, alleged reports of persons and their encounters with their own *Lebenswelten*, more elaborate stories of past human circumstance, exemplars of human character and images of human conduct. These message-bearing survivals may speak to us artlessly, in parables or in riddles; their voices may be clear, ambiguous or discrepant. They may purport to communicate useful information, advice or an effective image in which to express what we wish to say or wish to do. We may attribute authority to them or merely sagacity. They may be listened to, consulted, used, neglected or ignored. Since what they mean to us is whatever they may be made to mean, we are not concerned to determine their provenance in the past. Indeed, whether or not these survivals are scenes from a mythology, products of poetic imagination or alleged bygone exploits is often a matter of indifference. Their virtue is their familiarity and useful-ness. In short, they are *legenda*, what is 'read' and what may be read with advantage to ourselves in our current engage-ments.

These survivals, then, are constituents of a present, and here where it is a present of practical engagements, they are objects (like all others) accepted, understood in terms of their qualities and attended to in terms of their meaning and worth (if any) to ourselves in pursuing our current purposes, distinguished only in purporting to be voices from the past. They may have been lost and later recovered, but they become available to us in procedure, not of critical enquiry, but of recall to mind from where they lie scattered in our present or perhaps already assembled in the archive of a common vocabulary of practical discourse. Every society has an inheritance, rich or exiguous, of such survivals from past and to know one's way about it is a condition of articulate practical activity.

With us, some small part of this 'living' past is an actual or an imaginary ancestral past in which we locate ourselves, or more generally the society to which we belong. Or it is composed of objects, some stored in registries and record offices, whose messages are directly concerned with our present contingent identities and with the relationships of our current practical life: certificates, diplomas, contracts, testimonials, agreements, charters of incorporation and so on. And it is their authoritative character (their reference to future) which occasions their recall and which may make it worthwhile to corrupt the record, to see that it gets lost or to destroy it.

But for the most part the relationship between ourselves and this practical recorded past is conceptual, and the usefulness and the use made of these survivals in our current engagements is independent of any connection with our individual selves. It lies before us, a vast miscellany of recorded actions and utterances recognized as an almost inexhaustible source of analogies and resemblances in terms of which to express our understanding of ourselves or to interpret to others our purposes and actions. It extends the range, the vocabulary and the idiom of our self-understanding (or at least our self-image) by providing a gallery of familiar persons and situations with whom we may identify ourselves or with which we may identify our current circumstances. It offers a collection of allegedly well-known exploits which in approving, reprobating or excusing we may disclose our current allegiances. It reveals customs and practices which we may view with horror, with admiration or with indulgence and thus express or protest our own virtue. It provides relics which in venerating, respecting, disparaging or ridiculing we declare our own dispositions.

Knowing nothing of them except by hearsay, a man may protest the modesty of his attainments by disclaiming the wisdom of Solomon or of Solon. He may be accused of being 'medieval'; he may be said to have the touch of Midas or to have met his 'Waterloo'. A politician today may represent himself as a 'Moses' or a 'Cincinnatus'; or he may absolve himself from the inglorious niceties which belong to the character of Agag. The Huns and Vandals are always with us, Robin Hood is a deathless character and Canute an imperishable (although usually mistaken) warning. The self-respect of the British Grenadier is celebrated (in song) by being linked with the valour of Lysander. And images which have survived from this past may conjure up and perhaps reconcile us to our mortal condition:

Xerxes did die
And so must I.

In short, this is a 'living' past which may be said to 'teach by example',[2] or more generally to afford us a current vocabulary of self-understanding and self-expression.[3]

And when considerable passages of this recorded past have been assembled by putting together these fragmentary survivals they have been made to yield important conclusions about ourselves and our current circumstances; that it is a past which displays a 'progressive' movement to which our own times belong; that it exhibits a darkness to which our own enlightenment is a gratifying contrast; that it tells a story of decline and retrogression of which we are the unfortunate heirs. It is this past which is evoked in nostalgia; and unlike our encapsulated past it is one from which we may escape when we find it embarrassing.

This practical past, I shall argue, is not itself an 'historical' past, and consequently I must return later to investigate its character more critically and its claim to be, in any significant sense, 'past'. Meanwhile our business is to consider its status by considering the status of the practical present which is its counterpart.

4

This present–future of practical engagement, composed of subjects of a certain (optative) character related to one another in terms of their desires, purposes and actions and

---

[2] Lord Bolingbroke, *Letters on the Study of History*, II.

[3] I have purposely confined myself to the commonplace. But, although what may be won from the art and literature of a civilization goes far beyond anything to be identified as 'lessons' learned or with hackneyed and unrecognized quotes from Virgil, Dante and Shakespeare, it relates, like everything else, to the 'ordeal of consciousness'.

related also to objects, some of which may be recognized to have survived from the past and understood in terms of their alleged worth in the conduct of practical undertakings, is not a shapeless, unspecified encounter with the confusion of all that may be going on, nor is it a mere attitude. It is a coherent, self-sustaining understanding of the world in which a single formal character is imposed upon everything that receives attention.[4] It has a language of its own and it may be recognized as an autonomous universe of discourse. And large claims have been made on its behalf; namely, that it is itself the 'real' world, or that (at least) it is the 'primordial' and inescapable present.

Now, these contentions are important to us because they deny the possibility of an independent 'historical' past, and if they could be sustained they would frustrate any attempt to distinguish and specify such a past. For if (as I have argued) the modal character of past is the counterpart of the modal character of the present to which it is related, and if this present–future of practical engagement were the sole, unconditional, authentic present, then it follows that the past which is its counterpart (a recollected past composed of objects recognized to have survived and understood in terms of their worth in respect of a present practical enterprise) must be the only authentic past. And the expression 'historical past' could mean either this past (and thus become a redundant expression), or this past somehow corrupted or misconceived and so of no account.

The first and largest of these claims springs from a doctrine about 'human existence'.[5] A human being, it is

---

[4] The scale of such engagements may be large or small (seeking a so-called condition of 'salvation' has been included among them), and dignity and duty, as well as difficulty, may be considerations to be taken into account. And, of course, mistakes may be made in the attribution of conditional value or worthlessness to an object. But here, all objects are alike in being understood in terms of their alleged worth in relation to some undertaking.

[5] I refer to Heidegger and some others, rather than to more

alleged, is endowed with a capacity for free, 'transcendent', purposive activity, and his sole concern is to 'live'; that is, to seek and enjoy his identity in the exercise of this capacity. He belongs to a world – his so-called *Lebenswelt* – composed of others of his kind (to whom he recognizes himself to have a 'moral' relationship and to whom he may also be instrumentally related), and of objects which he necessarily and 'immediately' perceives in terms of their relationship to himself and his purposes. Given his alleged character (an active agent poised between birth and death and concerned only to pursue his self-chosen practical purposes) the meaning of everything he encounters, as of everything he fabricates and every action he performs, must be its propensity to illuminate, to promote or to hinder that pursuit. And this is not a character he reflectively imposes upon the objects he encounters, or one which in a procedure of enquiry he 'finds' to be that of some or all of them; it is their immediately perceived, unavoidable substantive character. Of course, deliberation may be required to determine the circumstantial worth of any of them in relation to a current engagement, but they have no so-called 'empirical' qualities, shapes, sizes, positions, etc., other than as components of this 'human world'. And if it should be suggested that there are universes of discourse other than this (that of 'art' or 'science', for example) the response is that these may be shown to be but disguised versions of this universe of practical engagement. They can have no independent status. In short, what is being asserted is the unconditionality and immediacy of the present–future of practical activity, the one on account of the other.[6]

---

commonplace pragmatists whose award of unconditionality to *praxis* is both arbitrary and obscure.

[6] Somewhat similar claims have, of course, been made on behalf of other purported universes of discourse. Lichtenberg (a chemist), in an engagingly speculative passage in his notebooks, wonders how he can reconcile himself to speaking the language

But this contention cannot, I think, be sustained. It is incontestable that a present–future of practical engagement, and the past which is its counterpart, composed of such subjects and such objects, is a coherent relationship of subjects and objects and an autonomous, recognizable and familiar universe of discourse, and not merely a 'point of view' or an 'attitude'.[7] But everything said about it, and all that may be said, announces it to be a conditional universe of discourse; what I have called a mode of understanding, specifiable in terms of the conditions which constitute its modality. And the contention that, in virtue of an all-embracing amplitude, it is a genuinely unconditional universe of discourse is supported only the by the claim that the objects which compose it are objects of 'immediate perception'. This claim is clearly false: an object understood exclusively in terms of its relation to some current human purpose is certainly not an object of 'immediate perception'. But even if this claim to 'immediacy' could be sustained, it would not be enough. For, although an object of 'immediate perception' (a mere 'this', a 'here' and a 'now') may perhaps be said to be unconditional, it escapes conditionality only on account of its extreme abstraction, insignificance and exiguity. And further, this large claim of unconditionality on behalf of the present–future of practical engagement suffers from the fatal defect of all such claims: it is self-defeating. There is no way in which it might be questioned, confirmed or refuted. For if this present–

---

of practical discourse when he knows that all that may be said in it is 'scientifically' false and therefore false. And Plato claimed unconditionality for 'philosophical' understanding in terms of which the objects which compose the present–future of practical engagement revealed themselves to be mere 'shadows'.

[7] The idiom of understanding concerned is aptly represented in the newspaper headline: '500,000 flee from £45 million hurricane'. Its pressure gradient is a recognition of its destructive force and its direction is an anticipation of its reaching a particular place on the map.

future were what it is here claimed to be, then this universe of discourse must itself be nothing other than an object of practical concern, and the engagement of making and elucidating this claim in respect of it can be no more or other than an action performed by the claimant in pursuance of a current practical purpose.

But if this attribution of unconditionality to the present–future of practical engagement and to the past which is its counterpart cannot be sustained, the lesser claim that practical understanding is 'primordial' and is an inescapable universe of discourse calls for consideration. The contentions here are that practical understanding is that in which a human being awakes to consciousness; and that, while other modes of understanding may be concerned with objects of other kinds than those which compose the present–future of practical engagement, such objects are conceptually constructed out of those which belong to practical understanding and unavoidably reflect the modality of the materials out of which they are constructed. In short, all modes of understanding have an intrusive, qualifying component of an original practical understanding which may never be excluded.

Now, it may be said (perhaps with some exaggeration) that practical understanding, as it has been specified, is a mode of understanding which precedes any other mode of understanding in the life of a human being.[8] In the confusion of all that may be going on we learn first to distinguish objects in terms of their worth to us in satisfying our wants (objects, generally speaking, of desire or aversion), and it is only subsequently that we may or may not learn to engage in other and more sophisticated modes of understanding. Moreover, this practical understanding

[8] What we ordinarily perceive rarely, in fact, has this absence of ambiguity: it is a much more messy affair in which we come and go somewhat inconsequentially between a variety of universes of discourse. And as for priority, some of our earliest experiences are not practical, governed by usefulness, but poetic and governed by delight.

may be recognized as unique in being universal to mankind and a condition of survival. Thus, the claim that it is in this sense the 'primordial' universe of discourse may (with some reservation) be conceded.

But it does not follow, when later perhaps we learn to engage in other modes of understanding, speak to ourselves and with others in other languages, assume different modal characters and concern ourselves with objects of a different modal constitution, that these objects are discerned in and abstracted from those which belong to the present–future of practical engagement. Indeed, it is logically impossible that this should be the case. For an object constituted in terms of one set of conditions cannot itself be transformed into an object which owes its character to a categorially different set of conditions. Nor can it be 'dissolved' so as to provide 'materials' from which an object of another sort might be conceptually constructed. In every determinate mode of understanding we go again to the confusion equipped with a set of modal considerations and unconcerned with what previously and in terms of other conditions we may have found there. Indeed, not to do so is to become entangled in a mixture of modes which spells total inconsequence. The so-called 'priority' of practical understanding and of the subject and objects which compose the present–future of practical engagement is at best circumstantial, not logical; in relation to other modes it is obtrusive, not intrusive.

Nevertheless, it will be said, this obtrusiveness is not insignificant. For it cannot be denied that every engagement to understand, whatever its modal conditions, is a practical performance; an action of an assignable agent occupying a station in a present–future of practical activity and eligible to be considered in these terms. Each such engagement emerges in a choice to undertake this enquiry and not another. Each 'takes time' and is an expression of a preference about how time shall be spent. Each looks to a future and recalls a practical past. Each runs its course marked out by the circumstantial fortunes of the agent: his health, the distractions he suffered and the favours he enjoyed. In short, each has a meaning as a constituent of the *Lebenswelt* of the agent concerned. Moreover, the products of all such engagements, whatever their alleged modalities, are records of how their authors spent their time; passages of biography. And these products (the written-down conclusions of this enquiry to understand the 'historical' meaning of Magna Carta, or this 'scientific' theorem) are objects launched into the present–future of practical activity, objects which occupy space, may be lost or destroyed, may perhaps be owned, sold and bought, are eligible to acquire an untold variety of use-values and are at the disposal of whoever may use them, for whatever purpose, in his own practical engagements. The manuscript of Hume's *Treatise* may be used to stop a hole to keep the wind away.

All this is unquestionable and must be insisted upon. But the conclusion we are often invited to draw – that on this account every engagement to understand is nothing but a practical activity governed only by the considerations which constitute the subject and objects in practical discourse – follows only if the larger claim of practical understanding to be genuinely unconditional understanding is conceded. But when it is recognized as a conditional mode of understanding and the present–future of practical engagement to be an abstract universe of discourse, room has been made for other and independent modes of understanding constituted in terms of categorially different conditions. No doubt a 'scientific' or an 'historical' enquiry moves towards its conclusions circumstantially from one day to the next, helped or hindered by the weather encountered by the *Beagle* or by the distractions suffered by the agent concerned, and all that constitutes it a passage in a *Lebenswelt*; it may even be said to be an 'immoral' enquiry which ought not to have been undertaken. But this is certainly not the procedure and these are not the considerations which constitute it a 'scientific' or an 'historical' enquiry. The subject who undertakes such enquiries, the objects or observations he is engaged to understand, the meanings he attributes to them and the conclusions he reaches are of a categorially different character from the subject, the objects of his practical concern and what he makes of them which together constitute the present–future of practical engagement. The *argument* of Hume's *Treatise* cannot be used to stop a hole to keep the wind away and a scientific theorem cannot be said to be either 'moral' or 'immoral'. And it is because this distinction is categorial that these universes of discourse, while they are incapable of denying one another, necessarily exclude one another.

As an engagement, then, the practical mode of understanding, and as the situation of a subject, the practical present–future, may be said to have a certain circumstantial priority, an undeniable and an almost continuous lien upon our attention, and a powerful resistance to being interrupted. And all other engagements may be recognized as holidays, enjoyed from time to time, from which we are recalled to the business of life and death and dinner and the mode of understanding these entail. But as categorially distinct modes of understanding they cannot be subordinate to practical understanding, the circumstantial priority of which gives it no superior status. Their relationship to it and to one another is conversational, not argumentative.

This recognition of practical understanding as a conditional mode of understanding and of the practical present as a conditional mode of present does no more than make room for other modes of understanding, each with its conditional present composed of a reflective subject related to modally distinguished objects. And my concern now is to specify an 'historical' mode of understanding. In relation to practical understanding it will doubtless appear as a holiday excursion, and those who undertake it may often find some difficulty in releasing themselves from the exigent demands of practical engagement. But its character as a categorially distinct mode of understanding lies, not in this circumstantial relationship, but in the conditions which specify it. And I propose, first, to consider 'history' in respect of its being a mode of understanding exclusively concerned with the past; that is, to consider the modal conditions which specify an 'historical' past. And since this past is the counterpart of a present composed of modally conditioned objects and of a procedure in which this past may be invoked from these objects, it is with the modality of this present that I must begin.

5

We begin, then, with a present. And what I mean by a present is a universe of discourse composed of a subject (that is, a reflective intelligence identified in terms of a mode of perception) related to objects (that is, things identified in terms of certain conditions): a subject and objects which correspond to and define one another.

Now, whatever else historical understanding may be, it is certainly and exclusively concerned with past. Practical understanding may or may not be concerned with past (and if it is, then that is only part of its concern), and aesthetic understanding is never concerned with past, but historical understanding is unique in being concerned only with the past. Consequently, the present in historical understanding is distinguishable as a subject exclusively concerned with past (an 'historian' as such) related to objects which speak only of past (that is, things understood exclusively in terms of their relation to past). This is the most general of the modal conditions of the present in historical understanding, and it is absolute.

More specifically, however, this present is exclusively composed of objects recognized, identified and understood as survivals from past; this is the condition in terms of which a thing may be an object of historical attention. The present in practical understanding is composed of objects distinguished and identified in terms of their worth in a current engagement to satisfy a want, and this is no less the case when they are also recognized to have survived from past; but the present in historical understanding is composed of objects recognized, not merely to have survived, but solely and expressly as survivals, vestiges, remains, fragments of a conserved past. Consequently, they are present objects which evoke past and are incapable of evoking future. Present here is present–past as surely as present in practical understanding is present–future. And I hope I have disposed of the contention that the present in historical understanding must be the present–future of practical understanding because the present of one who is an historian is also composed of objects understood in terms of their value in respect of his engagement. Certainly, such a man's present includes objects (such as the pen in his hand and the paper on his table) which are not understood as survivals from past but in terms of their current useful qualities. Certainly, an historian's engagement (as a performance) takes time and looks to a future when he shall have laid down his pen. But these are categorially irrelevant considerations; the present in historical understanding is exclusively composed of objects recognized as survivals from past.

This present is perhaps the most sophisticated of all presents, difficult to achieve and difficult to sustain. The conditions of abstraction (objectification) here are more severe than those of any other present. Thus, historical understanding is especially prone to relapse into some other engagement, and the objects which compose its present may easily be displaced in favour of others determined by other considerabilities and belonging to some other universe of discourse. And, of course, the insinuating voice of practical understanding, recalling us to a present, not of survivals from past as such, but of objects recognized in terms of their practical use, is the most seductive of all invitations to defect. Indeed, human beings lived long enough with only the haziest notion of an historical mode of understanding and with little incentive to learn, and it has been said (with some exaggeration) that even now such interest in past as we may have is confined to what it may be induced to tell us of future.[9]

Nevertheless, historical understanding is not a hopeless enterprise doomed to succumb to distraction. Here, as elsewhere, the circumstances of perception and the self-understanding of the subject may go some way towards promoting and protecting the integrity of the undertaking. Thus, a Roman coin turned up by a gardener's spade is likely to have an undecided character, circumstantially eligible to be recognized as any one of a variety of different objects. A mere curiosity? A saleable article? A 'treasure' for the boy? An object of historical enquiry? But just as the 'find' of a professional beachcomber is almost certain to be understood in terms of its practical worth, so the discovery of an archaeologist is likely to be an object of historical concern. And an object framed apart in a museum, a record office or even a family archive, a ruin, the record of a belief no longer believed, a defunct practice or rule of conduct, a legend without any current significance, or an object so worn or so out-of-date that its place in the present–future of practical engagement is manifestly exiguous – all these and their like are circumstantially defended against recognition in terms other than those of historical concern.

But this is a merely contingent consideration, to do with the emergence or not of an historical engagement. The character of history as a mode of understanding lies elsewhere; neither in occasions favourable to its appearance upon the scene nor in the acceptability of its conclusions, but in the conditions of understanding in terms of which its conclusions may be recognized as 'historical'

[9] 'History [sc. the past] is important to us only when it matters to us today. We have a sufficiency of histories that take up one or another item from the warehouse of the past for no better reason than that the item has thus far been allowed to lie about uninventoried.' This contention must, of course, be distinguished from the claim that there is no other kind of past than that which is of current practical interest.

conclusions. When this logical integrity is lost or compromised, all is lost.

The present in historical understanding, then, is itself a past; it is what is often called a recorded past, which means only a past which has itself survived and is present. It is composed of actual utterances and artefacts which have survived, which are understood as survivals, and are now present exactly as they were uttered or made except for any damage they may have suffered on the way.

But further, these utterances and artefacts, recognized as survivals, are recognized also as themselves performances; that is, as the utterances and fabrications of long-dead human beings, exercising such talents as they had, engaged in transactions with others, responding to what they believed to be their local situations, and expressing themselves, their thoughts and their beliefs. These recorded utterances may contain reports of what others than their authors are alleged to have thought or said or done, and descriptions of what is alleged to have happened. But such reports and descriptions are not read by an historian as informative utterances testifying (correctly or incorrectly) to what they report; they are constituents of the performative[10] utterances (addressed, not to posterity or to some future historian, but to contemporaries) in which their authors were responding to their current situations. And although some of these performative utterances may be notable for some *ex tempore* quality of wisdom, or (like the Athanasian Creed) have survived to occupy a place in a current present–future of practical engagement, this is no part of their historical character: they are what they are in terms of the transactions to which they belonged. In short, the present in historical enquiry is a recorded past composed of *res gestae* recognized as survivals.

For the most part, these survivals, recognized as performative utterances, belong to a bygone present–future of

---

[10] I use this word informally and without meaning it to evoke the intricacies of J. L. Austin's theory of 'speech acts'.

practical engagement; they are fragments of transactions in which their authors sought to satisfy their wants. This Minoan pot was made to cook a dinner or to carry water from the well, not in order to inform Sir Arthur Evans about a Minoan civilization which has not itself survived. This Dead Sea scroll is a confession of faith or the terms of a ritual, this Foreign Office telegram instructs an agent to speak and tells him what he should say, this charter endows this borough with certain 'freedoms' or 'immunities', this letter of Erasmus to Pope Leo X half-admits his illegitimate birth and pleads to be relieved of the disabilities this entails, and in this diary (perhaps written in a code) its author addresses himself. Their mode is that of present–future, and their survival to occupy the present of historical discourse does nothing to qualify this mode. And even when their alleged design was 'to put the record straight' they represent a practical concern with only a more distant future, a concern with reputation in the minds of a later generation. And whatever references to past they may themselves contain are to a more distant past recollected or recalled for its worth in diagnosing a present situation, devising a response to it, or expressing a then current practical self-image.

Not all the objects which compose the present of historical concern are mere survivals from bygone worlds of practical engagement. It contains also mathematical and scientific theorems, philosophical investigations, musical compositions, poems, works of art and so on. These also are *res gestae*, performances which have survived. But if there are to be genuine histories of science (as distinct from historical accounts of the place occupied by scientific engagement in a *Lebenswelt*), or of philosophical reflection (as distinct from 'the lives of the philosophers'), of music, art or literature, then these surviving objects must be distinguished in terms of the universes of discourse to which they belong and understood in terms of their appropriate modal provenances.

Historical enquiry, then, begins in a unique kind of

present composed of objects all of which are recognized as
bygone performances which have survived. It is a present–
past in which everything has had imposed upon it the
character of a survival and that of a performance whose
utterance may be difficult to interpret but which can be
neither true nor false. These artefacts and recorded utterances may be abstracted from the place they have come to
occupy in a current world of practical, or perhaps scientific
or artistic engagement, or they may be retrieved from
where they were let fall in bygone times by those who made
or used them, and often they lie scattered in a confusion
which reflects, not their characters, but the circumstances
of their survival. Each is a fragment, damaged, perhaps
mutilated, often detached from its transactional relationship with others or trailing relationships no less opaque
than itself. Nevertheless, an historian's only entry into the
past is by means of these survivals. And the first concern of
an historical enquiry is to assemble them from where they
lie scattered in the present, to recover what may have been
lost, to impose some kind of order upon this confusion, to
repair the damage they may have suffered, to abate their
fragmentariness, to discern their relationships, to recognize a survival in terms of its provenance, and thus to
determine its authentic character as a bygone practical or
philosophical or artistic etc. performance.

But a recorded past, composed of objects recognized as
res gestae which have survived and understood in terms of
their authentic characters, is not itself an historical past.
And this is not merely because it contains only those objects
which have happened to survive or because many of
them inevitably remain, in one degree or another, somewhat misty and imperfectly understood fragments. Even a
complete collection of carefully preserved and authenticated survivals of a certain sort does not itself constitute an
historical past. The nineteenth-century Statute Book is not
itself a history of nineteenth-century legislation. And the
assemblage of poetic utterances which compose the *Corpus
Poetarum Latinorum* is not itself a history of classical Latin

poetry, nor is this so merely because it may be conjectured to be incomplete. A recorded past is no more than a bygone present composed of the footprints made by human beings actually going somewhere but not knowing (in any extended sense), and certainly not revealing to us, how they came to be afoot on these particular journeys. Certainly, these survivals constitute an historian's present and are the only past upon which he can lay his hands, although even here his knowledge is not direct or immediate; but they provide nothing he seeks. For what he seeks – an historically understood past – is of a wholly different character: it is a past which has not itself survived. Indeed, it is a past which could not have survived because, not being composed of bygone utterances and artefacts, it was never itself present. It can neither by found nor dug up, nor retrieved, nor recollected, but only inferred.

An historically understood past is, then, the conclusion of a critical enquiry of a certain sort; it is to be found nowhere but in a history book. And it may be specified only in terms of the procedure of this enquiry. This is the theme of my next essay, but meanwhile it may be briefly identified as an enquiry in which authenticated survivals from the past are dissolved into their component features in order to be used for what they are worth as circumstantial evidence from which to infer a past which has not survived; a past composed of passages of related historical events (that is, happenings, not actions or utterances, understood as outcomes of antecedent happenings similarly understood) and assembled as themselves answers to questions about the past formulated by an historian.

I do not contend that an historical past is the only past, or that it is the only significant past, or even that it is the only past to be found in alleged pieces of historical writing. And what I have said does not require that there should anywhere be found a piece of writing which exactly reflects an imagination so relentlessly concentrated upon relating a passage of historical events in answer to an historical question about the past that it never diverges into a consideration, for example, of what it was 'like' to be within the walls of Constantinople in the late April of 1453 or to be a Pelagian in the Rome of AD 390, never breaks step for a moment to speculate upon the intentions of a philosopher or the motives of a politician, or never utters a practical judgement. In short, I have not been concerned to *prescribe* any particular interest in the past, but only to distinguish different modes of past in terms of the presents to which they are related and of the procedure in which they may be discovered or created.

There are some pieces of writing about the past which take no account of the distinctions I have explored (or, indeed, of any others) for which the past is just any old past, and which consequently remain regrettable muddles. There are others – works of prophecy or so-called prediction – in which the past is understood merely in terms of what it is alleged to foretell. There are others again, in which the past is a collection of exemplary occurrences. And there are many expressly or inadvertently devoted to making us acquainted with a past composed of *res gestae* and earn our gratitude for the liveliness they impart to these episodes. They (like all other engagements) are to be valued for what they provide and deplored only when they affect to provide what they do not provide. But there are others which (whatever else they may contain) exhibit the kind of enquiry and disclose the kind of past I have begun to distinguish as 'historical' and may consequently be recognized as, in this respect, engagements in historical understanding.

6

I have already noticed a past, which I have called a practical or useful past, which is often confused (and indeed sometimes identified) with an historical past. And I shall end this essay by reconsidering its character in order to distinguish it more exactly from an historically understood past.

It is clear that a practical past, composed of artefacts and utterances alleged to have survived from past and recognized in terms of their worth to us in our current practical engagements, cannot easily be confused (much less identified) with an historical past composed of passages of related historical events which have not survived, assembled as answers to historical questions about the past: they have nothing whatever in common. But this practical past may be, and often is, confused with the recorded past of survivals which is the present in historical enquiry. And I propose now to argue that this practical past, both in respect of the character of its contents and the procedure in which it is assembled, is wholly different from the recorded past of historical concern, and further that even its claim to be a genuine past is equivocal.

The objects, which in coming to compose the present of historical concern are identified as survivals from past, are unavoidably obscure. And this obscurity must be dissipated before they may be translated from performances which have survived into circumstantial evidence from which an historically understood past may be inferred. That something was made or uttered is evident in its survival, but exactly what it was may be ascertained only in an enquiry concerned to relate it to its provenance, and understand it in terms of its occasion. Thus, for an historian, a survival from past is a not-yet-understood object: in respect of being present it is an accepted fact but in respect of its being a survival from past its authentic character is a matter for enquiry.

Similarly, a practical present is, in part, composed of objects – artefacts and utterances – which are recognized to have survived from a near or a more distant past and are ready to be recalled from where they lie in the present, to be noticed, enjoyed or employed for what they may be made to mean or for whatever they may be worth in respect of current practical engagements. Such artefacts may include an ancient highway marked upon a map and inviting exploration, a 'medieval' castle, an old windmill, a ruin, monuments, relics, pictures and 'antiques' recognized by their design, which (to the instructed) may indicate a maker's name, or by a mark which assigns a date. And without any great sense of oddity we recognize a fossil found in a quarry to belong to this past of objects which have survived. Our bookshelves contain extended utterances which have survived from the past. Many words, brief expressions and sayings, their authors forgotten, have survived embedded in our vernacular of ordinary discourse; or, like the words reputed to have been spoken by Ruth to her mother-in-law, are recalled from where they lie in one of the great archives of past utterances. And it is with these survivals, which occupy so large a place in our practical present, that I am now concerned.

Record here is (so to say) the mirror image of the record which constitutes the present in historical enquiry. There, an artefact or an utterance is a puzzling survival from the past, a *factum probandum*. And the questions asked are: What is it? What was its provenance? What is its authentic utterance? Here, on the other hand, the puzzle is a current practical situation: What to think, to say or to do about it and what are the resources available to be employed in responding to it? And what, if anything, is recalled is not an opaque survival from a past of performances which may perhaps and with some difficulty be made to reveal its authentic character; it is a transparent item recalled, not from the past, but from where it lies in a perpetually accumulating collection of unmistakable present artefacts and utterances understood in terms of what it may be recognized to offer of worth in a current practical engagement. The question asked is not, What did this object or utterance mean in the circumstances in which it was made or uttered? or, What may it be made to report indirectly about a past which has not survived? but, What use or meaning has it in a current present–future of practical engagement? Indeed, with our attention fixed upon a puzzling present–future and upon the value here and now of whatever has been said or done in the past, it is often a matter of indifference to us where or when it may have been said or done, whether it stems from a legendary or a so-called 'historic' situation, or whether it was the voice of Zeus or Confucius or Shakespeare, the Duke of Wellington or Rip van Winkle which spoke. All that matters is that its utterance shall be unmistakable and usable.

What, then, is this so-called 'past' which hovers over us when we recognize these present artefacts and utterances to be objects which have survived? Certainly we may acknowledge ourselves to be indebted to their long-dead and usually unknown makers and authors, but this is no different from the debt we may owe to a contemporary who provides us with a useful artefact, an example of how we should behave, or a piece of sage advice about how to conduct our affairs. And if we ascribe some superior merit to what has survived simply in virtue of its having survived, we are not attributing to it a significant location in the past, we are merely accounting for its present useful-ness in terms of its durability. And were we to infer from these surviving utterances a past composed of teachers concerned to impart to us the lessons we now believe ourselves to have learned from them, or a past of artefacts designed for the use we now make or may wish to make of them, or even a past designed to impart information to us, then the inference would certainly be false. There is no such past. In short, this practical, so-called living 'past' is not significantly past at all. It is that part of a present–future of practical concern which is composed of objects recognized, not as survivals but merely to have survived, recalled for use from where they lie in the present and understood and valued for what they have to offer in current practical engagements.

And this view of the matter is, I think, confirmed when we consider the procedure in which this didactic and useful so-called 'past' is evoked from surviving record. It is perhaps commonly supposed that it emerges in a critical enquiry. An historian, it is suggested, perceives in surviving record a somewhat obscure performance and in a critical enquiry seeks its authentic utterance, thus making it available to convey to us whatever advice or wisdom that utterance may contain. And Machiavelli's recourse to the recorded past is recognized as a remarkably subtle and sustained engagement to cull from 'Roman history' important prescriptive messages for the rulers of his day. In short, it is suggested that these messages come to us from a past composed of historically authenticated performances which have survived. But this can hardly be the case.

The exploits which emerge from an historian's critical enquiry are bygone performative utterances whose ascertained authentic meaning lies in their unrepeatable conditions and in the wants and designs of agents who were alive and are now dead beyond recall. These survivals, in respect of their authentic characters, are complex and ambiguous identities, delicately balanced compositions of equivocal likelihoods. They could not endure detachment from their circumstantial conditions, and they can have no message for us. But what is capable of being enlisted to help us respond to our current situations is something quite different: emblematic characters and episodes, abstracted from record in a reading which divests them of their contingent circumstances and their authentic utterance; symbolic and stereotypic *personae*, actions, exploits and situations.[11] And they become available to us, not in a procedure of critical enquiry but merely in being recalled from where they lie, scattered or collected, in the present.

[11] When we were children, out for a walk in difficult country, tired and disposed to lag or to subside upon a grassy bank, my father used, half-seriously, to exhort us to further effort by invoking record: this, he would say, is not what Trojans would do. But Trojans were not long-perished people, the intricacies of whose lives, performances and fortunes only a critical enquiry could resuscitate from record; they were living and to us familiar emblems of intrepidity.

A record reputed to be a mine of prophetic utterances may be consulted at random, after the manner of the *sortes Vergilianae*; and here the yield is not advice but an alleged unavoidable destiny and the courage to accept it. The Old Testament, its character as the recorded past of the ancient Hebrew people ignored and belief in its alleged divine authorship suspended, has long been known as an un-equalled collection of exemplars of human character and situation and a rich vocabulary of verbal and situational images, of parables and analogies, in terms of which to understand, express and respond to current situations. And it was in 'Livy', a well-known collection of *legenda*, lying upon his table in Sant'Andrea in Percussina, and not at all in 'Roman history', that Machiavelli found the exemplars of human conduct which he used so effectively to identify current situations, to express his reading of what was afoot in his time, to predict what was likely to come of it and to counsel and admonish the rulers of his day.[12]

The didactic or so-called living 'past' is not significantly past at all. It is the present contents of a vast storehouse into which time continuously empties the lives, the utterances, the achievements and the sufferings of mankind.[13] As they pour in, these items undergo a process of detachment, shrinkage and desiccation which the less interesting of them withstand[14] and in which the rest are transformed from being resonant, ambiguous circumstantial survivals from bygone human life into emblematic actions and utterances either entirely divorced from their circum-stances or trailing similarly formalized circumstances: occurrences, artefacts and utterances, transformed into

[12] Livy is cautious about the founding of Rome, but Machiavelli, even if he is not quite 'like a boy who has newly read his Livy' (Harrington), neither has, nor needs to have, any hesitation about accepting it as a symbolic situation.

[13] Not unlike the storehouse which Ariosto's Astolfo found on the moon (*Orlando Furioso*, Canto 34).

[14] Such items may be said to belong exclusively to the recorded past of historical understanding.

fables, relics rather than survivals, icons not informative pictures.

Each item in this storehouse has been identified by a label, but there is no indication of how, if at all, they may be related to one another, and little or no significance is attached to the time when they were put into store: they are all equally 'processed' objects which have survived from an indeterminate past. There is no official custodian and the place is in considerable disorder. From time to time, however, it appears that persons have retired there and have spent many happy hours turning over the lumber it contains. In many cases they are little better than vulgar rag-pickers, fascinated with junk. But some (Herodotus or Geoffrey of Monmouth) have a good eye for interesting or colourful or curious objects and these, disjoined from their circumstances, they have arranged on shelves cleared for the purpose. Moreover, it has got about in the world of current enterprise that this storehouse contains items of genuine usefulness (which, indeed, have been processed in order to be useful), and a counter has been set up at the back door where people may come and ask these self-appointed librarians of *legenda* for what they want. Sometimes enquirers will ask to spend an afternoon routing round for themselves in the hope of picking up a bargain. And parties of schoolchildren will be shown round by their teachers. Those who have become knowledgeable about the contents of this storehouse have published lists and even descriptive catalogues of interesting items available. In one way or another there is considerable, though uneven, familiarity with what it has to offer.

There are some well-known items which are so often used in the world outside that they may be said to be on permanent loan to the present of practical engagement. In this respect the contents of the storehouse constitute a vocabulary of practical discourse. Here are Cain and Abel, Moses, Horatius, Caesar crossing the Rubicon, Athanasius at Nicea, Canute on the seashore, King Arthur, Wilhelm Tell, Luther at Worms, Nelson putting his telescope to his blind eye at Copenhagen, Robin Hood, Captain Oates, Davy Crockett, and here is Colonel Custer making his last stand. This vocabulary of symbolic characters (ill-distinguished from mythical figures and from such images as sturdy oaks, snakes in the grass, and the burdensome Albatross) contains emblems of all the virtues, vices and predicaments known to mankind, continuously added to and continuously recalled for use.

Sometimes a search of this storehouse will yield something more closely and usefully linked to our practical engagements. It may disclose a purported authority for doing what we want to do, a precedent for taking a certain course of action, a warning or an encouragement. It may provide a document purporting to prove that I am a forgotten descendant of the late Duke of Portland and heir to a vast fortune hidden in the vaults of Baring Brothers, and it is here we may hope to find the 'original contract' legitimizing a current government. Indeed, for an object to be found in this storehouse confers upon it such prestige that people have been known to forge them, smuggle them in when no one is looking and then ask for them in a year or two. Moreover, this storehouse has acquired such a reputation as a collection of potentially useful objects that there is now a whole profession of persons who, for a fee, will rummage through it on your behalf, coming up perhaps with the disconcerting or gratifying news that you are somebody quite other than you supposed yourself to be.

In short, the contents of this storehouse are altogether different from the recorded past of performances, artefacts and utterances, in which an historical enquiry begins. It is not a collection of exploits but of emblems; not evoked in a procedure of critical enquiry into the authentic character of a not-yet-understood survival, but merely recalled as unproblematic images; and valued, not for an historically understood past which may be inferred from them, but for their present usefulness.

For example, Bismarck, in the course of a famous speech on 14 May 1872, said, 'Nach Kanossa gehen wir nicht' (using the princely plural). And in doing so he had resorted to the storehouse and had taken out the item labelled 'Canossa', just as another (on a different occasion) might take out 'Washington crossing the Delaware' or as Karl Marx took out 'feudalism'. But what Bismarck took out was not that obscure exploit of genuine or simulated penitence performed by the Emperor Henry IV in a northern Italian hill town in the hard winter of the year 1077 when he and Pope Gregory VII were locked in dispute about certain high ecclesiastical appointments and property in the Imperial realm, an occurrence composed entirely of contingent beliefs and local circumstances. *That* could never have been of the slightest interest or use to Bismarck or his audience. What he took out was not 'a bit of history', nor even an item from the recorded past; it was a relic, an emblematic trope in terms of which to express and to dramatize his position *vis-à-vis* the Pope in the so-called *Kulturkampf*.

Or again, and this time a frustrated resort to the reliquary. Not long ago a barrister in a court of law referred to a passage in Magna Carta (C.39) to the effect that a free man shall not be arrested, imprisoned, disseised of his freehold or otherwise disadvantaged except by lawful judgement of his peers. And he argued that his clients, five black men, should therefore be tried by an all-black jury. He invoked a thirteenth-century document which has survived. But his appeal was not to an historically understood recorded past, an utterance whose authentic meaning is hidden in long-defunct local circumstance. *That* could have no message or authority to impart to the court he was addressing. What he sought was something that could be represented as a relevant and persuasive analogy to support his case. In plumping for Magna Carta he was astute: as a storehouse of emblems of just procedure it has long been credited with almost magical authority. In choosing C.39, however, he made a careless mistake. If it had mentioned a jury, that, no doubt would have been enough for his purpose. The historical consideration that it would have meant, not a modern jury, but a collection of neighbour-witnesses reputed already to have intimate knowledge of the accused and of the alleged offence, would not have deprived it of all analogical value. But in order to be useful what is recalled must have some plausible resemblance to the situation to which it is to be related; and this recourse to the storehouse of emblems miscarried because neither in this passage nor elsewhere has Magna Carta anything whatever to say about the composition of juries.

Those who have recourse to this collection of alleged past performances reduced to exemplary characters, utterances and situations may, then, make mistakes; but they are mistakes of an entirely different kind from those to which an historian is liable in seeking the authentic character of a survival. And this difference is illustrated in their different valuations of forgeries. A forgery is valuable in an historical enquiry only when its authentic character as a forgery is recognized; here it is valuable only when its authentic character is *not* discovered. Moreover, this collection of symbols is valued in respect of the support it may give to what is recognized to be a desirable present of practical engagements, and when it is found to be valuable we say that 'history is on our side'. But it may contain items which are not only worthless but recognized to be positively injurious and therefore proper to be forgotten or even proscribed. The removal, for example, of the name of Trotsky from the official Bolshevik emblematic past or that of the explorer Stanley from the practical past of Zaïre was part of an undertaking to construct a symbolic vocabulary of practical discourse which would not prejudice an approved practical present. But those who promoted these suppressions were not tampering with or rewriting 'history'; they were merely removing what they regarded as useless or noxious items from the reliquary in which a practical 'past' is preserved, an enterprise long known in China as 'the rectification of names' and a commentary upon the mutability of human circumstances.

What I have called a practical past is, then, a present of

objects recognized to have survived. It is an indispensable ingredient of an articulate civilized life. But it is categorially distinct both from the survivals which compose the present of an historical enquiry and from an historically understood past which may be inferred from them. It is an accumulation of symbolic persons, actions, utterances, situations and artefacts, the products of practical imagination, and their only significant relationship to past is not to the past to which they ambiguously and inconsequentially refer but to the time and circumstances in which they achieved currency in a vocabulary of practical discourse.

II   Historical Events

The fortuitous, the causal, the similar, the correlative, the analogous and the contingent

1

Historical enquiry may be recognized in terms of often vague but not wholly insignificant marks of identity which distinguish it from some other enquiries with which it might be confused. And perhaps the most obvious of these characteristics is an exclusive concern with past. But the expressions 'historical enquiry' and 'historical understanding' may acquire an explicit meaning only when they stand for a categorially distinct mode of enquiry and understanding and when the conditions of this mode are specified. And I have opened my exploration of these conditions by assuming that they will include a reference to past and by considering in general terms the character of a distinct kind of past which may be appropriately identified as an historical past. I do not suppose myself to have proved that an historical past must be of this character. Nor have I stipulated this kind of past to be an historical past. But to those who, perhaps because of what they have encountered in pieces of alleged historical writing, are inclined to identify an historical past, also or alternatively, with that no less categorially distinct kind of past I have called a practical or a didactic past, I have replied as follows. First, that I am not dismayed when I find both kinds of past represented in a history book, because it is not to be expected that any book will avoid being somewhat miscellaneous, but that we are concerned here solely with the 'history' in history books. And to insist that an historical enquiry may properly be concerned with both these kinds of past is not merely to give it a wider range of legitimate concern, but to fasten upon historical understanding the character of a categorial confusion. And secondly, I have said that, since a practical past is not itself genuinely past and is not the product of a critical enquiry about the past, it may be identified as an historical past only at the expense of denying to historical understanding a genuine concern with past and depriving it of the character of a critical enquiry about past – a somewhat extravagant undertaking.

I propose now to explore the thesis that an historical past is composed of passages of related events, inferred from present objects recognized as survivals from the past, and assembled as themselves answers to historical questions about the past. The questions which call for consideration are: What is an historical event? What is the procedure of enquiry and inference in which historical events may be elicited from a present of survivals? What is the character of the relationship which may subsist between historical events and in terms of which they may constitute a passage of events?

2

An historical enquiry emerges in a concern with a present composed of objects recognized, not merely to have survived, but as themselves survivals; that is, recognized not as relics invoking veneration, as utterances of notable wisdom or foolishness, as currently useful artefacts or as objects of contemplative delight, but as things in respect of their being vestigial. They are present objects which speak only of past.

Secondly, these objects are recognized to be themselves exploits, human doings which have been performed, utterances which have been pronounced, artefacts which have been made, fragments of the bygone purposive engagements of their perhaps unknown authors which have survived (although sometimes recognizably damaged) and are themselves now present. This is the unmistakable character of some of these objects. They are human expressions which (whatever may be inferred from them) purport to record only themselves as exploits performed. Other such objects may be writings which purport to chronicle, describe, report or refer to the doings of their authors other than that of the utterance itself, or to the doings of other persons, and perhaps also to happenings which are not themselves human exploits but which occupy a place in the world of human doings in respect of being happenings which evoked responses in actions or utterances: a particular eclipse of the moon, the eruption of Vesuvius which submerged Pompeii, the Lisbon earthquake which entered so deeply into the intellectual life of eighteenth-century Europe, the departure of herring from the Baltic, or the French agricultural disaster of 1693. Nevertheless, the character of these surviving utterances as informative reports about human performances or about other kinds of happenings is subordinate to their character as themselves the performances of their reporters; it merely specifies their artefactual idiom. Here, what is reported (no less than the reporting of it) is an exploit, the performative utterance of its reporter.[1] There are (so to say) no 'neutral'

[1] The character (and not merely the accuracy) of the information which such compilations as the Doomsday Book or the *Valor Ecclesiasticus* of 1535 purports to supply is related to the intentions of the compilers; what is reported in official *fasti* (a monastic or a royal chronicle, or even an account book) is related to its purpose; and this is also the case with more informed reports. In 1595 the Duke of Feria 'reported' to Philip II that 'Naples, Sicily and Milan

or unconditional reports. In short, the present of historical enquiry is composed of artefacts and utterances recognized as survivals and understood as themselves *res gestae*.

Thirdly, the pre-eminent voice of such an artefact or utterance may be recognizable as that of a determinate universe of discourse: it may be recognized as a musical composition, a philosophical argument, a scientific theorem, a religious ritual or a contribution to a political debate. And in this respect it is an object related to a particular kind of historical past: that of musical composition or of practical engagement and so on. But none of these objects which compose the present of historical concern has an exclusive character or speaks with a single voice. And in virtue of its heterogeneous utterance each is eligible to be used in a variety of historical enquiries some far removed from that suggested by whatever may be recognized as its pre-eminent voice.

This, for historical enquiry, is the character of the Gospel according to St Mark, a Persian carpet, Hobbes's *Leviathan*, the Anglo-Saxon Chronicle, the score of *Figaro*, a parish register of marriages, Fountains Abbey, a field path or a song. Each is a *res gesta*, an exploit which was performed in bygone times and has survived exactly as it was performed except for the damage it may have suffered on the way. And each is an oblique source of information which may be used in seeking answers to a variety of historical questions about the past, but was certainly not designed to supply any such information.

A survival as it may come to us, with perhaps little in the way of a significant context, is something of a mystery surrounded by mystery. But it may attract our attention in appearing to be in some respect intelligible and interesting.

---

flourish as never before under their present government.' But the purpose of the 'report' was to persuade Philip that he should engage himself to bring England under that same government (F. Braudel, *La Mediterranée.et le Monde Mediterranéen à l'époch de Philip II*, I, p. 449).

And without imposing upon it some other character than that of a survival from bygone times, it may be naively accepted as what it purports to be – a not wholly mysterious fragment of a recorded past, an anecdote of human circumstance.[2] And this, or perhaps a little more, is all that we may be disposed to ask of it. But for an historian it is an object which provokes enquiry: for him, a recorded exploit, whatever its immediate interest or intelligibility, is something not yet understood.

The more distant concern of this enquiry is, no doubt, to infer from recorded exploits a past composed of historical events related in answer to an historical question; that is, to transform surviving exploits into evidence to be used in the composition of a past which has not survived because, being a past of events and not of exploits, it could not have survived. But its immediate concern is with the further determination of the recorded exploit itself.

Since this enquiry is about an object understood to be itself a performance (and not a proposition about a performance) the question, Is it true? cannot arise. And to ask, Did it happen? or, Was it performed? is either to ask the only question which has already received an answer (an artefact of some sort is certainly present), or it is to beg the only question which still demands an answer, namely, What is it? What is its authentic character? And this question means something more than, Is it what it purports to be? For although it may be important to determine whether or not the object is a counterfeit performance (such as one of Thomas Wise's forgeries, or the Piltdown Skull) it is not deprived of an authentic utterance if that is what it turns out to be. The important historical consideration is not that an object which has survived from the past may be

[2] For example, the cryptic MS fragment dug up on the north shore of the P'uch 'ang Sea in 1908: 'The Tatar girl addresses you. Since we parted I went westward, and whenever I remember the days we spent together my heart is heavy. I write this letter in haste and time allows only a few lines. The heart is broke by absence.'

deceitful but that it is certainly conditional. The design of the enquiry is to extend our understanding of what it is by exploring its conditionality: that is, to understand it as an *ob-ject*, a something in particular that in bygone times has been thrown into the world. And every such extension of this understanding is not merely something added to whatever has been ascertained; it is a 'revision' of the character of the performance concerned.

The present in historical enquiry is, then, composed of performances which have survived, and the first engagement of such an enquiry is to distinguish and understand these performances in terms of their connections with others to which they may be circumstantially related. The principle of this enquiry is that everything is what it is in respect of such relationship; and its procedure is one in which recorded exploits are made to interpret and criticize one another. There is no independent criterion of their historical authenticity.

Every such performance has a language, and to understand it in these terms is an important stage in the enquiry. To discern the exact shapes which comprise its design, to recognize the vocabulary and syntax of its utterance, the images used and the symbolism employed is to relate it to a practice of conduct, of belief or of understanding, and what is being sought is its character in terms of its subscription to the conditions of a practice. But since practices (languages) are encountered only in performances (utterances) and may be elicited only in a procedure in which performances are understood and related in this respect, the enquiry in which the language of a performance may come to be understood is also an enquiry in which the language itself is discerned. A dictionary or a grammar of the language of Christian symbolism at any time, or of the sixteenth-century English vernacular, is comprised of inferences from actual utterances. In short, the language of a performance is a certain sort of relationship it has with other performances and is one component of its conditionality.[3]

[3] Every performance which has survived may be said to have a

A performance, however, is never merely a subscription to a practice. It is also a substantive action or utterance which belongs to a transaction and seeks a satisfaction; that is, a future. And the authentic characters of performances which have survived are what they are in terms of their transactional relationships with others, and they may emerge only in an enquiry in which they are made to interpret and criticize one another. For example, some part of the conditionality of a performance may be resolved into the questions, who? when? and where? which may be answered with a name, a date and a place. But such answers are merely shorthand for a collection of not-yet-understood survivals among which some may be discerned to be transactionally related to it. And these other performances are not the 'scene' in which it took place, or the 'background' against which it was performed, or even its 'context'; they are the conditions which constitute its character, just as it is among the conditions which constitute their characters.

Historical enquiry, then, begins in a present composed of objects recognized as exploits which have survived; each is a fragment of a bygone present composed of *res gestae*. This present is continuously enlarged by the discovery of hitherto unknown survivals and by the recognition of the vestigial character of objects hitherto known only in some other terms, such as their current usefulness. The immediate concern of the enquiry is to understand performances recognized as survivals in terms of the transactional relationships which constitute their characters as performances, to discern their conditionality and thus to determine the 'authenticity' of their utterance. How arduous an undertaking this may be will depend on the opacity of the

---

'language' in this sense. Not only Harrington's *Oceana* (the language of which has been identified as that of 'civic humanism'), but also the ancient Greek ship and its cargo discovered under the sea at Kyrenia in 1967, and the Risen Christ of Piero della Francesca in Sansepolcro.

object, its relative detachment in survival and many other considerations. But it may never be dispensed with: no object which has survived yields its authentic character to mere observation, and its worth in further historical enquiry depends upon an understanding of its authentic character. And it may never be definitely concluded. Indeed, no small part of this enquiry is properly devoted to finding better reasons for accepting a current interpretation or good reasons for modifying it. It is in this manner that an historian himself creates his present, his so-called 'sources', and endows them, not with 'authority', but with 'authenticity'. Thus understood a record never lies; even if it does not mean what it says it may be made to say what it means. All roads lead somewhere. And in this enquiry an historian has no extrinsic destination of his own; he merely wants to know where the road leads.

3

To have learned to read a survival critically, to have recognized its universe of discourse, to have come to understand its 'language', to have discerned the conditionality (that is, the authenticity) of its utterance, to have repaired the damage it may have suffered, and to be able to defend one's conclusions in argument, are themselves considerable achievements. And there (or thereabouts) the enquiry might stop, the surviving object itself remaining the centre of what is nevertheless an historical focus of attention. But for an historian even inherently interesting surviving fragments of past (and certainly the vast bulk of what has survived when it is understood in terms of its authentic utterance) are not the end of an investigation but the beginning of an enquiry concerned, not with what they are, with their characters as performances, but with what may be inferred from them about a past which has not survived. And I propose to consider, first, this enquiry when it is directed to eliciting from surviving record a past constituted of occurrences which are not themselves performances and which have not themselves survived.

Briefly, by an historical occurrence I mean an identified condition of human circumstance or transactional relationship of human beings alleged and understood to be what actually happened, in a certain respect chosen by an historian, then and there, not itself an artefact or utterance which has survived, nor a performance, but the net outcome of divergent and perhaps conflicting performances: an anatomized fragment of past circumstances. It is the conclusion of an enquiry designed to infer from surviving utterances and artefacts what they do not and cannot themselves tell him, namely, what has not itself survived but did in fact happen.

But since no such occurrence can be understood or even identified singly and in isolation (each being what it is in relation to other occurrences), the unavoidable concern of this level of historical enquiry is with exploring and anatomizing the characters of situations of various dimensions composed of related occurrences distinguished in such terms (broad or narrow) as the enquiry finds to be appropriate to the characters it has attributed to their component occurrences. An historical occurrence is a rudimental historical situation, and an historical situation is a composition of notionally contemporaneous, mutually related, historical occurrences.

Historians denote the situations they undertake to explore or the characters they attribute to the situations they have explored sometimes in relatively neutral terms and sometimes in terms which reflect something of their conclusions. Thus: Pauline or Edessan Christianity,[4] the *Völkerwanderung* of the third and fourth centuries, Alexandrian Platonism, 'the Epic poetry of the early middle ages',[5] 'the formal structure of English feudal society around A D

[4] A. Nock, *St Paul*; F. C. Burkit, *Early Eastern Christianity*.
[5] W. P. Ker, *Epic and Romance*.

1200',[6] 'marriage in Christian history',[7] 'the civilization of Renaissance Italy',[8] 'a sketch of English public law at the death of Henry VII',[9] 'the Reformation in Zürich', 'the scientific revolution', 'the *mentalité* of Affective Individualism in seventeenth century England',[10] 'the condition of England in 1685',[11] 'the Scottish Enlightenment', 'the tyranny of Greece over Germany',[12] 'the French Revolution', 'Jeffersonian democracy', 'logical positivism'. These alleged conditions of human circumstance and their like are commonplaces of historical imagination. They are not themselves artefacts or utterances which have survived, such as those which compose the present of an historian; they are not the designs, purposes or exploits of assignable agents; and they are not, and do not purport to be, expressions which denote the self-understandings of persons who occupied these situations. They are the unintended outcomes of various and divergent designs and actions to which the vanquished no less than the victors in the transactions concerned have unintentionally and unknowingly contributed. They identify situations (composed of mutually related occurrences) as the subjects or the conclusions of an historical enquiry, and what falls to be considered is the character of the enquiry in which they may be made to emerge and come to be historically understood.

An historical situation is, then, a coherent structure of mutually and conceptually related occurrences abstracted from all that may have been going on there and then and made to compose an answer to an historical question about a past which has not survived. It is the conclusion of an historical enquiry. Such a conclusion must, of course, be

---

[6] S. F. C. Milsom, *The Legal Framework of English Feudalism*.
[7] C. N. L. Brooke, *Marriage in Christian History*.
[8] J. Burckhardt, *The Civilization of the Renaissance in Italy*.
[9] F. W. Maitland, *Constitutional History of England*.
[10] L. Stone, *The Family, Sex and Marriage in England, 1500–1800*.
[11] Thomas Macaulay, *History of England*, ch. 3.
[12] E. M. Butler, *The Tyranny of Greece over Germany*.

derived from surviving, authenticated artefacts and utterances; there is no other source of information or back
entrance into a past constituted of situations which have
not survived. Nevertheless, it cannot be composed of a
collection of surviving records, and it cannot emerge in a
procedure of 'letting the records speak for themselves'.
And this is not at all because we cannot 'trust' their
utterances, or suspect that they may be 'partisan' or
'corrupt' or in some way unreliable 'accounts' of the past,
but because a record is a *res gesta* and its authentic utterance
is nothing but the performance it constitutes. Nor may an
historical situation be derived from what surviving records
may be alleged to report or give an account of. Such reports,
also, are themselves the bygone performances of their
authors; they may not be 'false', but in respect of an
historical situation their utterances are certainly oblique. A
survival is not a witness to an occurrence whose testimony
may be believed or doubted and (if found trustworthy)
adduced in support of a reading of an historical occurrence.
And so-called 'discrepant' reports are not 'jarring witnesses' to an occurrence between which a choice must be
made.[13] Indeed, the 'discrepancies' of records and of the
reports they are alleged to contain are nothing other than
their characters as different *res gestae,* and the observation
that 'as raw materials for history, the gospels have the
gravest deficiencies, they are in places discordant' is
absurd. In short, an historical enquiry begins, not with an

[13] 'An editor of no judgement, perpetually confronted with a
couple of MSS to choose from cannot but feel in every fibre of his
being that he is a donkey between two bundles of hay. What shall
he do now? Leave criticism to critics you may say, and betake
himself to any honest trade for which he is less unfit. But he
prefers a more flattering solution: he confusedly imagines that if
one bundle of hay is removed he will cease to be a donkey.' (A. E.
Housman, *Preface* to Manilius)
 The question, 'Can we believe Gildas?' (R. G. Collingwood and
J. N. L. Myres, *Roman Britain and English Settlements,* p. 432) is
unfortunately phrased.

endowment of so-called 'direct' and perhaps 'unreliable'
evidence about the past which has not survived, but in a
present of performances which have survived, which
speak, but which do not address themselves to the questions an historian is concerned to answer: 'witnesses'
whose 'evidence' relates only themselves. Indeed, the
historical virtue of a survival is precisely its lack of pretence
of being historically informative. Its value lies in what
Housman called its 'purity'; that is, the clarity with which
it reveals (or, in a study of its provenance, may be made to
reveal) its authentic utterance as a performance which has
survived from bygone times. And since there is nothing
that may properly be called 'direct' evidence of a past which
has not survived, the engagement of an historical enquiry
cannot be that of learning to distinguish between the
relative credibility of different 'accounts' of the past or that
of 'filling the gaps for which no direct testimony exists'.

But if an historian's present of artefacts and utterances
which have survived provides him with nothing that may
be recognized as 'direct' evidence of bygone situations
which have not survived, this does not stigmatize historical
understanding as irreparably defective. Such survivals may
be made to provide something which, so far from being an
inferior substitute for 'direct' evidence, is much more to the
point and more reliable; namely, circumstantial evidence of
a past which has not survived. Thus, an enquiry concerned
to assemble a bygone situation which has not survived is
not concerned to assess the veracity or the credibility of
what are mistaken for accounts of it or of its component
occurrences; it is concerned with the validity of the conclusions inferred from the surviving artefacts and utterances
and particularly from all that is contingent to, and uncompromised by, their performative character. For an historical
situation is the conclusion of a procedure of inference in
which surviving record is transformed from a performance
into circumstantial evidence for a past which has not
survived.[14] And this is a very considerable transformation.

[14] Albert Schweitzer's *Quest of the Historical Jesus* is a matchless

The focus of attention here is not upon the authentic utterance of the surviving object (the Rosetta Stone, the Gospel of St Mark, a portrait of Alphonso II, Ulm Minster, the Njal Saga, Descartes' *Discourse* or the Statute of Uses), but upon what it may incidentally disclose, upon its asides, what it lets fall, what is there but is not part of the design, what it may be perceived to take for granted and upon what it leaves unsaid. [15] And the importance of the recognition of the authentic utterance, the 'purity', of a survival lies in the guidance this gives to the interpretation of these incidental disclosures. In short, in this enquiry every survival is an heterogeneous object, without any exclusive reference or utterance and eligible to be drawn upon in constructing a variety of historical situations, each an answer to an historical question about the past. It is whatever an historian may find in it to his purpose. Thus, there may be legal, political, economic, philosophical, musical or scientific situations; that is, situations constituted in terms of a recognizable universe of discourse. But there are no such exclusive surviving objects.

No doubt what I have called an historical situation suffers from its relative isolation, and it is important that it should not be claimed to be more than it is, namely, a situational identity abstracted from all that may have been going on then and there. But its historical value lies in its distinctness and in the extent to which the relationships and convolutions of its component features have been explored and anatomized: Namier's *Structure of English Politics on the Accession of George III*, or Edwyn Bevan's *Jerusalem under the High Priests*. The past which is the product of this level of

---

critical review of a century and a half of engagements of varying quality to infer an historical situation from what has survived in record.

[15] Inference *e silentio* is notoriously speculative, but in intellectual history, where what is not said may circumstantially be recognized as intentionally not said, its yield has been great.

historical understanding is a past composed of patterned situations of various dimensions, durations and constitutions, each a patch of illumination surrounded by the darkness of a past which has not yet been thus understood. As the conclusion of an enquiry an historical situation is what it is alleged to be only in respect of the evidence upon which it relies and of the procedure of inference it employs. There is no other source of information, no other and superior procedure of enquiry, and there is no independently known past to which it may be compared and in terms of which it may be tested or validated. If a *revenant* were to appear, to offer himself as an eyewitness or as a participant and were to say: 'It was not like that but like this', he would be recognized as only one more, somewhat odd, survival whose utterance has to be translated from the idiom of exploit into the idiom of evidence. Such an historical enquiry may, of course, err and its conclusions are always conditional, but it is not to be thought that, on this account, what I have called an historical situation is a fanciful construction or a matter of so-called 'subjective' opinion. It is an argued invitation to imagine the intricacies and the coherence of a condition of human circumstance which has not survived.

The genuinely historical limitations of this level of historical understanding remain to be considered, but I will notice now what I take to be a misconceived manœuvre to repair what is a misconceived shortcoming. It is often said that this engagement to anatomize historical situations is a superficial undertaking yielding only a past composed of insignificant glimpses of isolated, half-understood episodes and that it cannot resist reduction to a more profound enquiry. And it is suggested that this superior sort of enquiry is one which looks beneath the surface and is designed to disclose situations of human engagement, not as compositions of mutually related occurrences, but in terms of the operation of regularities which are not themselves occurrences: trends, or even what is alleged to be an underlying, perhaps economic or psychological, structure. But, while an enquiry of this sort may perhaps be a possible intellectual adventure, it cannot be recognized as a superior kind of enquiry capable of superseding the historical engagement to infer situations composed of mutually related occurrences from surviving record. Indeed, they are not even genuine competitors. Whatever intelligibility a situation may acquire from being understood in terms of a 'structure of communication', of *le cadre primordial des réalités économiques*, of 'the deeper regularities of human behaviour', of alleged 'permanent forces in history' or of 'long enduring factors' emancipated from circumstance, it is certainly nothing that could be inferred from surviving record.

Thus the enquiry of an historian who distinguishes a *mentalité* in terms of occurrences, of actual beliefs, of hopes, dispositions, sympathies and expectations entertained, of conventions practised, of procedures followed and of actions performed, all inferred from surviving record, can have no place for understanding it in terms of the regularities of so-called psychological processes or of the 'structure of a collective mind set'. And when Burckhardt in his *Griechische Kulturgeschichte* adduces what he calls *der Griechische Geist*, it is an historically valuable notion because it is an assemblage of related beliefs, attitudes, persuasions, habits, characteristic responses and so on inferred from recorded utterance. But it would be historically worthless if it were represented as a phenomenon of so-called 'collective psychology', or as some subterranean inspiration, or as an extra-terrestrial Intelligence brooding over actual belief and conduct and invoked to 'explain' what was said and done. It is not that human conduct must in principle be taken to occlude regularities (other than self-imposed circumstantial practices), or even that there may not be some brooding providential Intelligence that accounts for them; the point is that these considerations do not mix with and cannot take the place of an historical understanding concerned with what was actually the case, there and then, in terms of situations composed entirely of mutually related occurrences inferred from record.

4

A past composed of carefully anatomized situations of various magnitudes, durations and constitutions, themselves composed of mutually and conceptually related occurrences, is certainly a past which has been endowed with a certain level of historical intelligibility. And, so far as it goes, the enquiry in which such a past is inferred from record cannot be denied the character of an historical enquiry. But although it has been called the most sophisticated understanding of the past, it is, I think, an unstable level of historical understanding. It recognizes (or half-recognizes) what it cannot itself accommodate, and it cannot defend itself against being superseded by what is a genuine competitor, critical of it in its own terms, and thus capable of superseding it.

An historian who constructs a road-map of the Carolingian Empire *c.* AD 800 calling upon whatever records or half-obliterated survivals may serve his purpose, one who spells out the character of Elizabethan Puritanism or of a doctrine identified as 'civic humanism', who unfolds 'the structure of English politics on the accession of George III', or who (like Fernand Braudel) specifies the 'energy resources' of Europe in the late eighteenth century and computes them in terms of total 'horsepower' – such an investigator purports to be anatomizing a bygone present situational identity in terms of its constituent occurrences. No doubt he recognizes himself to be concerned with a passage of time which contains genuine change; but his enquiry, centred upon the articulation of a situational identity, cannot properly accommodate this recognition. Changes may be avowed, but only to be put on one side as insignificant; they make no difference to the so-called paradigm. Here, an historical past is composed of solid 'achievement', of 'results' and of situations understood in terms of their 'permanence'.[16] The only change an historical situation thus understood can accommodate is some minor shift in its tensions, some small displacement which does not compromise the situational identity. Indeed, an historical enquiry thus oriented will be disposed to seek situations of almost structural immobility, and to find them either in situations so brief that they may be represented as in fact changeless, or else (like Fernand Braudel) in situations so extended and anatomized on so large a scale (*la longue durée*) that they display almost 'geological' stability.

And further, an engagement to anatomize an historical situation, in specifying its duration recognizes it as an emergence and admits its evanescence; but the enquiry is not concerned to abate the mystery of its appearance upon the scene, to investigate the mediation of its emergence or to trace the vicissitudes of its evanescence. It is concerned only with correctly inferring an intelligible structure composed of notionally contemporaneous mutually related constituent occurrences. Of course, no historian engaged upon such an enquiry supposes that the situation he is concerned with emerged *ex nihilo* in a 'big bang', and he knows that to attribute its coming into being to 'the deeper regularities of human behaviour', to 'progress' or to the operation of *yin* and *yang* will not serve to make it historically more intelligible. But if, as is likely, he thinks that in order to accomplish his design some reference should be made to the mediation of its emergence, then all that his enquiry can properly accommodate is some suggestion of a 'pedigree', some recognition of an antecedent conceptually related situation which may be said to anticipate or forecast the situation with which he is concerned, but which plays no part in his understanding of it.

These, then, are what I take to be the historical defects of

[16] I have taken these words and this characterization of historical situations from Maitland's remarks on 'constitutional history' (*The Constitutional History of England*, pp. 526–39).

an enquiry concerned to infer from record a past composed of situational identities: transitory passages of human engagement represented as patterned situations composed of mutually related occurrences which come and go but are here halted and made to gyrate in a notional interval between coming and going. Of course, any past which is to acquire an intelligible historical identity must be abstracted from the flux and inconsequence of all that was going on then and there, and this procedure of abstraction is recognized when an historical past is specified as an answer to an historical question; but here immobility and the exclusion of all but conceptually determined relationships are added to the abstraction.

And the remedy for the shortcomings of this level of historical understanding is not, I think, in doubt. It lies in an enquiry designed to assemble a past, not of anatomized situational identities composed of mutually related occurrences, but of historical events and the conjunctions of historical events. And this is what I shall call an historical enquiry properly speaking.

5

By an historical event I mean an occurrence or situation, inferred from surviving record, alleged to be what was actually happening, in a certain respect, then and there, and understood in terms of the mediation of its emergence; that is, understood as an *eventus* or outcome of what went before. And since what went before is also understood to be itself composed of nothing but historical events, the historical character of an event is the difference it made in a passage of circumstantially and significantly related historical events. Thus an historical past may be said to be composed of passages of related events of various dimensions, durations and constitutions assembled in answer to an historical question: a past constituted not in terms of its situational immobility but of time and change.

This past is certainly distinct from all others in terms of its character and of the procedure in which it may be assembled, and it has perhaps an obvious claim to be recognized as a uniquely 'historical' past. It is not composed of a collection of utterances and artefacts which have survived. It is not a bygone present–future of human engagements and presented as an account of what that bygone present–future was in the conditional understanding of those who participated in it: what is sometimes called a past as it understood itself. Nor is it a past composed of anatomized immobile situational identities, the unintended (but not necessarily unobserved) outcomes of transactional encounters. On the contrary, what I have called an historical past properly speaking is an unqualified past, a past understood in terms of its past; that is, conditions of human circumstance come upon from behind and understood in terms of their emergence. It is the conclusion of an enquiry in which an historian infers a past composed of related historical events assembled in answer to an historical question, a past of which there can be no record and one necessarily unknown in default of such an enquiry.

Thus far, it may appear that what I have called an historical event is no more than a somewhat extended understanding of what I have called an historical situation, an understanding which may emerge from an enquiry designed to account for the occurrence of an already understood situation by attaching to it a past alleged to have promoted its appearance upon the scene. This, however, is a mistaken view of the matter both in respect of the character of an historical event and of the enquiry in which it may be inferred from record.

First, the engagement in an historical enquiry is not merely to account for the occurrence of an already understood situation; it is to understand a perhaps anatomized but a not yet understood situation and to do so in a particular manner, namely, in terms of the antecedent events to which it is significantly related. And secondly, the only past to which a situation alleged to be already understood might be related in order to make its occurrence more intelligible is a foreshortened past composed of occurrences in respect of their being recognized to have a conceptual affinity to the already identified features of the situation. And an engagement to seek such a past is a denial of historical enquiry. It commits the historical fallacy of *nunc pro tunc*, where the *nunc* is an already understood situational identity and the *tunc* is some sort of 'pedigree' alleged to account for its already known features. Thus, for example, an occurrence identified as the abolition of the British slave trade, 1806–7, may no doubt be made more intelligible by attaching it to a past which conceptually reflects this identification (a past composed of slavery, the trade, the activities of its opponents, etc.), but this will not endow it with the character of an historical event. What *that* requires is for the situation itself to be transformed by being understood as the outcome of an uncovenanted circumstantial confluence of vicissitudes which will certainly include events which had nothing to do conceptually with slavery or the trade.

An historical event, then, is not an assignable performance, and therefore it cannot be understood in terms of the intentions of a performer, his disposition, his beliefs, his reasons for acting or its so-called appropriateness as a response to his circumstances. And it is not what I have called an historical situation; that is, the transactions of notionally contemporaneous agents and associations of agents responding differently to recognizably common (but differently assessed) circumstances and made to compose a situational identity. It is not the consummation of a 'trend'; trends, no doubt, may be discerned, but only in backward glances and in stories whose end is already known. Nor is it the product of engagements, struggles, exertions and so on designed or apt to procure it as an outcome. It is a by-product of a past composed of antecedent events which have no exclusive characters, no predetermined outcomes and no inherent potentialities to issue in this rather than that, but which an historical enquiry may show that and how they have in fact done so. This antecedent past is not an 'incubator' in which subsequent historical events are 'hatched',[17] or an off-stage dressing-room where they await their call. It is itself composed of nothing but events, the circumstantial outcomes of conjunctions of events discerned in the same sort of enquiries. And an historical past, composed of passages of related historical events assembled in answer to an historical question, is the product of an enquiry concerned, not to account for or to explain the occurrence of already understood events, but to understand their not yet understood characters; that is, to understand *what* they are in respect of their relation to antecedent events.

What this view of the matter denies or excludes I shall consider shortly. But, at one extreme, it does not deny that human engagements and associations are composed of the actions and utterances in which assignable persons express their self-understandings and choose and seek the satisfaction of their wants. Nor does it suggest that there is any impropriety in seeking to understand these performances in terms of the dispositions, intentions, beliefs or reasons of those who act and speak. Indeed, it recognizes that such enquiries about performances (which may attribute responsibility or blame to assignable persons or convict them of error or delinquency) are both possible and eminently interesting to us even when they are not designed to elicit information or advice about how to conduct ourselves in our current engagements. It merely recognizes historical enquiry, properly speaking, to have a different concern; namely, with the unintended eventual by-products of such transactional engagements which,

[17] 'The century 1815–1914 is conveniently pictured as a century of comparative peace. Another way of seeing it, grimmer but perhaps more instructive, is as an incubation period' (A. Rappoport, Introduction to Clausewitz, *On War*).

because they are not assignable performances, cannot be understood in terms of 'personalities' but which may be understood in terms of their relation to antecedent by-products of human engagements. And it is agreed that such an understanding of the past is useless, and may be positively misleading to us in responding to our present circumstances.

And, at the other extreme, it does not deny that what has happened, is happening and shall happen may perhaps belong to some progressive or regressive movement, nor that there may perhaps be a diabolical or providential 'dialectic' in which all that happens contributes to some cataclysmic conclusion or to a 'far off divine event'. It merely attributes to historical enquiry a different engagement: that of composing a past in terms of continuities and convergencies of obliquely related historical events properly inferred from a past which has survived. It is an exact engagement, vulnerable neither to the accusation that it should be doing something other than what it purports to be doing, nor to the contention that it cannot resist reduction to some other sort of enquiry, but only to the criticism that on this or that occasion it has not in fact, and for some assignable reason, accomplished what it set out to achieve.

Four further considerations may be noticed. First, an historian's engagement to compose an historical event by understanding it in terms of the devious mediation of its emergence and displaying it as it was actually 'woven',[18]

[18] This is a Rankean word, misleading only when it is taken to imply a weaver, like the 'Fates' weaving the destinies of men. Ranke had a variety of expressions for what is being sought in an historical enquiry, and the most frequently quoted – 'Zeigen wie es eigentlich gewesen ist' – suggests that the historian already knows *what* happened and seeks only to understand its occurrence. But it is partnered by others which point in a different direction, e.g. 'was eigentlich geschehen ist'. The two perhaps may be combined in some such expression (not Ranke's) as: 'Zeigen wie es eigentlich zustande gekommen ist'.

may begin as a further enquiry about what I have called an anatomized situational identity. But it does not need to do so: there is nothing in historical enquiry which imposes upon it the character of a critical examination of an already explored and understood historical situation or makes this a necessary stage in an historian's engagement. If, however, it should do so, the upshot will be a transformation (not a confirmation) of the alleged character of the situational identity. Coming to understand an historical situation as an historical event is not merely adding to our situational understanding of what was happening; it will be a radical 'revision' of it.

Secondly, historical enquiry is not, strictly speaking, an explanatory engagement in which reasons are sought for past events being as they were. There is no *explanans* of a different character from an *explandum*: a 'law', a 'cause' or a propensity. Historical events are themselves circumstantial convergencies of antecedent historical events; what they are is how they came to be woven.

Thirdly, there are many considerations which may make even the most carefully composed historical event a somewhat tentative construction subject to revision. The discovery of hitherto unknown survivals, the critical reinterpretation of already known record and overhearing in it hitherto unheard or unheeded asides – these and their like are the occasions of what is properly to be called the 'rewriting' of an historical past. But historical events are immune to the criticism of the future: an earlier event cannot be made more historically intelligible in terms of later events. It is, of course, true that earlier happenings may acquire new characters on account of later, as Ruth *post mortem* acquired the character of an ancestor of King David; and in virtue of hindsight (that is, of our acquaintance with later happenings) earlier happenings may earn new meanings. But these cannot be historical characters or meanings.[19] Certainly it is the case that 'many sentences will occur in

[19] Historically, a fuller understanding of the career of Bismarck cannot come from the hindsight of one familiar with the later

historical writings which give descriptions of events under which those events could not have been witnessed',[20] and that an historical enquiry is not concerned to display a past situation merely as it was 'witnessed' to occur or as it was understood by its participants; but such descriptions are historically relevant only if the 'unknown' events which they invoke are significant *antecedents* to the situation the enquiry is concerned to understand historically. To have achieved an historical understanding of Cromwell or Napoleon may enlarge an historian's imagination, but it cannot be invoked as evidence from which to infer an historical understanding of Augustus Caesar. Nor is an historical past composed of a passage of related events like a *novelle*, full of hidden fatalities, and in which the meaning of earlier events becomes known only in relation to later and all events must await the *dénouement* for their true meaning to be revealed. It has no plot, much less a 'dialectical' order.

And further, it is often remarked that an historian in seeking to understand a passage of the past will invoke his current experience of the world and his beliefs or those commonly held by his contemporaries. Gibbon's understanding of Marcus Aurelius and of Theoderic is said to be 'modelled' on the benevolent despots of his day, and his interpretation of Christianity in ancient Rome is said to reflect the critical attitude of the 'Enlightenment'. Both Hume and Ranke are reputed to understand the past in terms of their different universal beliefs about human nature which they shared with some of their contemporaries. And this is said to be both unavoidable and historically valuable: an historical past must always be at least something of a reflection of the contemporary world of an historian. Is not Maitland's suitor to the Gloucestershire Assize Court in the twelfth century, with the disputed chicken under her arm, a convincing historical occurrence

---

history of Germany; it comes from such an enquiry as that of Otto Hintze in *Die Hohenzollern und ihre Werke*.

[20] Arthur C. Danto, *Analytical Philosophy of History*, p. 61.

because it reflected the life and the disputes of the English countryside in his own day? The suggestion that 'in the last analysis, whether consciously or not, it is always by borrowing from our daily experiences and by shading them, where necessary, with new tints that we derive the elements which *help* us to restore the past'[21] is both ambiguous and exaggerated; it does not recognize that these current experiences may as often be hindrances as they may be helps in seeking an historical understanding of the past. But at least it does not commit us to the absurdity of assigning them a place in the procedure of inference which constitutes an historical enquiry. In short, what is attributed to Gibbon and other historians is neither inevitable nor a virtue but a likely defect which every genuine historian consciously seeks to avoid. This, however, does not diminish the small but not insignificant value of any well-observed situation, past or present, as a source of suggestion about what to look for in composing a conjunction of historical events and in the education of the imagination of an historian.

Lastly, it may be thought that this account of historical enquiry as an engagement to discern the character of events in terms of the vicissitudes of their emergence condemns it to the frustration of an interminable search for a beginning. And this, perhaps, would be the case if such an enquiry pretended to be definitive or to be concerned with genuine origins. But it has no such pretensions. This is not a dilemma posed by the character of historical enquiry but a question which concerns the scale of an historical enquiry, and it is one which an historian must decide for himself. For the gift of historical understanding is nothing so remote of possible achievement as a seamless web of related events, nor anything so simple as events truly inferred from surviving record, and it has nothing to do with origins. It is the gift of an opportunity to understand a passage of the past in terms of hitherto unrecognized

---

[21] Marc Bloc, *The Historian's Craft*, p. 44 (my italics).

conjunctions, convergences and relationships of events and thus to imagine it more distinctly and perspicuously.

6

Where an historical enquiry is recognized as an engagement to assemble a past composed of events, themselves passages of related events, historical understanding expresses itself in a 'relation' of historical events, whether or not it is set out in a strictly chronological order, or takes the form of narration, or is composed in some other style. And there is a variety of ways of relating such a story, some no doubt better than others, in which an historian may reveal his capacity as a composer.Nevertheless, if such a composition is to be a recognizable passage of historical past, the relationship ascertained and employed must be of a kind which acknowledges and does not conflict with what is related. And what falls now to be exactly considered is the kind of relationship which may subsist between and may specify the characters of identities recognized as historical events. This, indeed, may be said to be the central question in any account of historical understanding. And I propose to consider it now from one point of view and to take it up from another point of view in the next essay.

An historical enquiry engaged to compose a past in terms of a passage of related events is necessarily concerned to ascertain and employ what may be called significant relationships; that is, relationships between antecedent and subsequent events which actually specify the characters of the subsequent events and in terms of which we may come to understand what in fact they are historically. This kind of relationship is often called an internal or intrinsic relationship, and it is contrasted with a merely external, coincidental or fortuitous relationship. For, 'chance' is not a total absence of relationship, or one which is merely unpredictable; it is a relationship which signifies something (perhaps something in respect of the occurrence of a happening), but nothing in respect of the character of what is related. Thus, historical understanding has no place for fortuitous relationships. And for an historian to present an occurrence as merely fortuitous is a confession of his inability to go any distance towards transforming it into an historical event. But this exclusion of 'chance' relationships from an historical past does not deny that occurrences do have fortuitous relationships; it means only that an historical enquiry, as an engagement to compose (as far as it may be possible to do so) a passage of significantly related events in answer to an historical question, has no place for the recognition of such meaningless relationships.[22]

But this concern with a past composed solely of significantly related events does not imply that every event is ideally related in this manner to every other event, or that an historical enquiry, designed to transform occurrences into events, is incomplete unless a significant relationship with all antecedent events is ascertained. It means only that no historical event is without a significant relationship with some other historical events. And it means, once more, that historical understanding is not a metaphysical engagement but a conditional undertaking to seek and to establish actual significant relationships between events by inference from record, in an enquiry capable of doing this and no more than this.

The position, then, is as follows. The attention of an enquiry designed to understand the character of an historical event in terms of the mediation of its emergence (this mediation being itself composed of nothing but events) is necessarily directed to antecedent events and to their antecedence. Since, however, mere antecedence, even if it were comprehensive, is clearly not itself a significant relationship, the engagement of the enquiry must be to

[22] In the writings of Machiavelli and others the word *fortuna* denotes an extraterrestrial will-like force to which may be attributed the mere occurrence of happenings which, having occurred, may or may not be eligible for transformation into historical events significantly related to others.

distinguish among these antecedents a passage of events which may be recognized to be significantly related to a subsequent: to detect the significant in the merely antecedent and thus to transform a subsequent into some kind of a consequent. How may an historical event be related to antecedent events in such a manner as not merely to account for its occurrence but to specify its character?

7

I shall make a beginning by considering the claim that the significant relationship between historical events sought in an historical enquiry must be a causal relationship. And it is appropriate to begin here, not merely because causal relationship is reputed to be the exemplar of all significant relationship, the sovereign release from chance and accident, but also because the word 'cause' has acquired a secure place in the vocabulary of historical discourse and is the most common expression for the kind of relationship an historian seeks and hopes to establish between historical events. And no doubt these two considerations are not unconnected.

The terms in which this claim is usually set out are substantially different from those I have employed to specify the character of an historically understood past, and they suggest that (whatever its merits as a mode of enquiry) it should not be confused with an historical mode of enquiry. And this indeed is one of my conclusions. But without anticipating this conclusion, I must set out the claim in its own somewhat confused terms.

The contention to be considered is that an historical enquiry is a concern to understand or explain reliably reported bygone occurrences and situations (here often miscalled 'events') and that this purpose may be achieved only in an investigation which seeks to understand them in terms of their causes or causal conditions. And it is further claimed that all other kinds of explanation are inferior to this kind, and must in the end surrender to a causal explanation.

There are two distinct versions of this contention. In the first an historical enquiry is said to be an engagement to explain reported bygone occurrences or situations by understanding them as examples of the operation of universal 'laws' or regularities which it is the task of the enquiry to ascertain and formulate. These happenings may be of various dimensions: 'the French Revolution', 'the Alaskan Gold Rush of 1898', 'the execution of King Charles on 30 January 1649 in Whitehall'. And although the terms in which they are reported and circumstantially identified will unavoidably display them as mixtures of particularity and genericity, the 'laws' used to explain them are not merely extrapolations of the circumstantial generalities: 'revolution', 'gold', 'execution'. Or alternatively it is claimed that the past which comes before us to be explained may be identified as a continuous flow of reliably reported occurrences and situations vulgarly called 'the course of history'. And the task of historical enquiry is that of transforming it into what is called 'the historical process' by understanding it in terms of a 'law' or 'laws' of historical change. In both cases, the 'law' adduced is said to represent the 'true forces' generating historical change and to be the cause of the reported occurrences. And an understanding of an occurrence in terms of these universal causal conditions is said to supersede and to be capable of taking the place of all other understandings.

The position here is that the past which is present to us and is available as an object of historical enquiry is composed of reliably reported (or perhaps recollected?) bygone occurrences or situations: the Emperor Henry IV in a posture of penitence at Canossa in 1077. Persons of an inconsiderable urge to understand may recognize such an occurrence in terms of whatever circumstantial intelligibility it may have, or they may impose upon it a character which corresponds to their ideological convictions. But others (namely historians) may embark upon an enquiry to understand its 'true' character: the difference between an historically understood situation and a reported situation is one of truth and error or illusion. The design of this enquiry is to reveal such a situation as an example of the operation of a universal 'law of history', or (alternatively expressed) it is to ascertain its cause. Thus it is said that 'an historical work only completely fulfils its task when occurrences unfold themselves upon its pages in their full natural necessity'.[23]

As an account of an historical enquiry this suffers from an obvious initial defect: it misconceives the character of the present–past with which an historical enquiry must begin. This present is said to be composed of reliably reported bygone occurrences or situations which have not themselves survived, and these reported happenings are said to be ready and waiting to be understood as examples of the operation of 'laws'. Whereas, the present–past in which an historical enquiry must begin is composed of obscure performances (artefacts and utterances) which have survived; and the occurrences and situations, said here to be awaiting explanation in terms of 'laws', are the conclusions of inferences from these survivals used as circumstantial evidence for what has not survived. And one of the consequences of this mistake is that this account of the procedure of an historical enquiry ignores all that part of it concerned with authenticating these survivals, transforming them into circumstantial evidence of something other

---

[23] Leon Trotsky, *History of the Russian Revolution*, I, p. 18. This, of course, is a modernistic description. But a parallel to it may, perhaps, be found in Augustine's mature view of *sacra historia* (the past as the story of Redemption), which terminated with the birth of Christ, and the 'truth' of whose component recorded occurrences was discernible only to prophetic insight. The whole of the past is constituted of what God has done, often through human agency; and sacred history is composed of that selection of occurrences in which God has expressed his redemptive purpose (R. A. Markus, *Saeculum: History and Society in the Theology of Augustine*).

than themselves, and making these inferences. At best we are given here only a grossly attenuated account of an historical enquiry. However, let us suppose an historian to have at his disposal such a circumstantially identified occurrence or situation. What then?

His alleged task is to discern its 'true' character by coming to understand it as an example of the operation of a 'law of history' or a 'law of historical change'.[24] In order to perform this task he must equip himself with such a 'law' or 'laws'. And he is said to do this in a procedure of examining (and perhaps comparing) a number of such occurrences and situations and coming to perceive them as structures composed of regularities. But this, also, is clearly a mistake: no such conclusion could issue from this procedure. What this 'historian' needs and what he must devise for himself is a collection of systematically related abstract concepts (such as those which constitute a science of mechanics or genetics) in terms of which to formulate 'laws'. How he may set about this enterprise we need not enquire; nor need we deny the possibility of his formulating some, perhaps 'sociological', laws. But what is certain is that they cannot be laws of 'history' or of 'historical change' because they do not and cannot relate to the circumstantially reported situations he designs to explain, but only to model-situations abstracted from them in terms of these 'laws'. In short, the distinction between such a model-situation (explicated in terms of regularities) and a circumstantially reported situation is not a difference of truth and error: it is an unresolvable categorial distinction. And whatever the defects and inadequacies of a bygone situation understood in the terms in which it was reported to have happened they cannot be redressed by putting in its place a model-situation abstracted from it. A situation recognized as 'an errand-boy on a bicycle in Hyde Park in

[24] This task is often made more obscure by being confused with that of discerning the 'true', law-determined, intention (here often miscalled 'motive') of an agent in performing what is said to be a reliably reported action.

1910' may be reported and understood in all its circumstantial detail, and somebody equipped to do so may abstract from it a model mechanical situation (a parallelogram of forces), a model physiological or biochemical situation, a model economic situation (an example of the disposal of scarce resources), maybe a model sociological situation, and any number of other law-formulated situations, but none of them, nor all of them put together, is a superior historical understanding capable of superseding and being recognized as the 'truth' or the cause of the reported happening: a 'law' cannot itself sustain the character of a cause. The whole exercise is nothing more than a pretentious muddle.[25]

The second version of this claim is more circumspect: it has nothing to say about an 'historical process' or about 'laws' of historical change or development. It is an undertaking, first, to spell out exactly the logical structure of causal explanation; and secondly, to sustain the thesis that an historical enquiry, as an engagement to establish a past composed of significantly related antecedent and subsequent events, must be an enquiry of this kind.[26]

[25] There are some unqualified examples of this kind of enquiry into the past, particularly in relation to a past identified in so-called 'economic' terms. And of course there may be harmless asides in this idiom in any piece of genuine historical writing. But its character and propensities are, perhaps, best revealed and illustrated where it has invaded and corrupted what, differently formulated, might have been a genuinely historical enquiry. For example, the recent exploration by a number of writers of the hypothesis that seventeenth-century Europe (and particularly the middle decades) displays a situation of 'something like general social–revolutionary crisis' which suggests the question, What was its cause? and provokes answers in universal terms.

[26] This claim has been argued, with marginal differences, by Carl G. Hempel in an essay called 'The Function of General Laws in History' and in the writings of some other of the contributors to Patrick Gardiner (ed.), *Theories of History*. And it may also be found in Karl Popper's *The Poverty of Historicism* and elsewhere in his work.

A causal explanation is said here to have three ingredients: an observed object, identified in terms of its kind, whose existence is to be explained; some other observed objects, also identified in terms of their kinds; and a universal 'law' (capable of being empirically falsified) which states that there is a constant, regular or systematic relationship between the existence of the kind of object whose existence is to be explained and the existence of these other kinds of objects, thus identifying them as its causal conditions and allowing its existence not merely to be observed but to be deduced. In respect of the universal 'law' invoked in this enterprise of explanation, the contention here is no more than that some such universal statement of relationship is a necessary premise for the recognition of a causal relationship between an object and other objects. Consequently, it is no part of the business of this enterprise to formulate, to validate or to falsify such 'laws'; it is concerned only to use such of them as are ready to hand and as may appear to be reliable and appropriate in the circumstances. They may be the conclusions of 'scientific' enquiries designed to formulate and to test them, or they may be plausible (perhaps trivial) generalizations about the kind of object concerned. And although they are a necessary ingredient of any argument concerned to establish a causal *nexus*, they may be tacitly assumed and not necessarily cited. In short, true of false, such regularian statements are a necessary ingredient of the logic of this kind of explanation; and they must be empirically true, although they may be trivial, if the explanation is to be convincing.

It may be conceded that this account of the logical structure of a genuinely causal explanation as a 'deductive –nomological explanation' delineates the conditions of a possible sort of enquiry and specifies exactly the kind of conclusion it is capable of sustaining. But the contention we have to consider is that an historical enquiry concerned to compose a past of significantly related events must be (or must surrender to) an enquiry of this sort. And for it to be recognizable as an even plausible model for an historical enquiry some adjustments have to be made in this account of causal explanation.

First, the object whose existence is to be causally explained and the objects invoked as its causal conditions must be recognized, respectively, as a circumstantially reported bygone happening identified in terms of its kind, and as circumstantially reported antecedent happenings identified in terms of their kinds and separated from it by an interval of time. This is a difficult adjustment, not easily absorbed, because of course causality itself knows nothing of any such interval of time. Secondly, the purpose of the exercise here is not to deduce the existence of an already empirically observed kind of object by joining it to its causal conditions, but to retrodict the occurrence of an already reported kind of happening by relating it to antecedent happenings recognized as its causal conditions, the premise of this recognition being an expressly or tacitly invoked universal 'law'. This 'law', of course, is not a 'law of historical change', but it may be expected to be the conclusion of a psychological, perhaps an economic or a sociological enquiry not concerned to explain occurrences but to formulate regularities; or it may be a reliable, 'reasonably well confirmed by empirical evidence', though perhaps trivial, generalization about human nature or circumstance or identified kinds of human behaviour.

This claim is set out as follows by Hempel.

> The explanation of the occurrence of an event of some specific kind E at a certain place and time consists, as it is usually expressed, in indicating the causes or determining factors of E. Now the assertion that a set of events – say, of the kinds $C_1, C_2 \ldots C_n$ – have caused the event to be explained, amounts to the statement that, according to certain general laws, a set of events of the kinds mentioned is regularly accompanied by an event of the kind E. Thus the scientific [sc. the historical] explanation of the event in question con-

sists of (1) a set of statements asserting the occurrence of events C_1 . . . C_n at certain times and places. (2) A set of universal hypotheses, such that (a) the statements of both groups are reasonably well confirmed by empirical evidence, (b) from these two groups of statements the sentence asserting the occurrence of event E can be logically deduced.

And in a marginally different formulation Popper contends that the design of an historical enquiry is to explain why a given event E occurred. This, it is claimed, must be a causal explanation or remain inadequate; and 'to give a causal explanation of an event means to deduce a statement which describes it, using as a premise of the deduction one or more universal laws, together with certain singular statements, the initial conditions'. These 'initial conditions' are, of course, specifications of the antecedent or accompanying events which, when related to E in terms of universal laws, are recognizable as its causal conditions.

This account of the procedure of an historical enquiry and of the character of an historical past is, however, muddled and untenable. And the objection to it is not merely that it absurdly purports to set out a model of so-called 'scientific' enquiry and explanation to which all enquiries must conform on pain of being pronounced inadequate or even invalid. Nor is there any substance in the commonplace objections that we lack the kind of generalizations upon which this model of explanation depends; or that, because general law-like statements do not have this place in historical understanding, they therefore have none. The objection is that it denies the elementary conditions of an historical enquiry as a concern to compose an answer to an historical question by assembling a passage of the past constituted of related events which have not survived inferred from a past of artefacts and utterances which have survived.

According to this account of it, an historical enquiry begins from a statement describing an 'event' of a certain kind and reporting it to have occurred and from similar statements describing and reporting the occurrence of other accompanying or antecedent 'events' of certain kinds; and its task is to deduce the occurrence of the one by relating it to the occurrence of the others in terms of universal laws which disclose this relationship to be causal. But this is not a possible procedure for an enquiry concerned to understand a not yet understood past which has not survived, and its conclusion is not of a kind that any historical enquiry, or any alleged historical enquiry, has ever sought.

First, an historical enquiry declares its concern with the past and effects an entry into the past by beginning in an observed present–past composed of objects recognized as survivals from the past which, when authenticated, are to be used as circumstantial evidence for constructing a past which has not survived. And if this causal enquiry were to begin (as it is alleged to begin) with an empirically observable past, then it must start with this present–past of survivals. But its alleged concern to explain the occurrence of such a 'given' (survived) past would condemn it to the secondary engagement of explaining the survival (that is, the occurrence in the present) of these survivals. And in order to avoid this absurdity, it affects to perform the impossible feat of leaping directly into a past which has not survived by beginning in a present of alleged informative statements reporting and asserting the occurrence of certain kinds of happenings, for example the defeat of the Napoleonic armies at Waterloo and its attendant circumstances ('initial conditions'). It then concerns itself solely with establishing a causal relationship between these descriptive statements of occurrence by invoking universal laws.

Secondly, this so-called 'event of a kind E', and the other 'events' reported to accompany it, are not what they are said to be; namely already described and understood kinds of happenings of various dimensions whose contextual relationship to one another and whose occurrence have been reported in statements which may be, or already have been, confirmed by 'empirical evidence' (whatever that may mean), and await only deductive proof of their occurrence. If they are anything at all, they are understandings of the characters of bygone situations which have not survived and the conclusions of inferences from the circumstantial evidence provided by what has survived, awaiting transformation into historical events. Thus, what must be the main concern of an historical enquiry – to understand the character of a not yet understood passage of a past which has not survived – is dismissed as a nugatory engagement in favour of a design to raise the occurrence of an alleged already described and understood kind of happening from the status of a report to that of a retrodicted necessity. And this attenuation of an historical understanding is inherent in the attribution to it of the character of a causal explanation. A cause may be sought only for an already known and understood effect. Here, both the 'events' which are recognized to be the causal conditions of the 'event' whose occurrence is to be explained, and the 'law' in terms of which they are recognized as causal, may be distinguished from all the events which accompany it and from inappropriate 'laws' only in terms of the character already attributed to the 'event' whose occurrence is to be explained. In short, it assumes to be already known what it is the purpose of an historical enquiry to ascertain.

Thirdly, an historical enquiry is here represented as a concern, not even with the occurrence of reported happenings understood in all their circumstantial complexity (mixtures of particularity and genericity), but only with the occurrence of happenings abstracted and identified in terms of their kinds. And this departure from the design of an historical enquiry also follows from the attribution to it of a causal character. A cause may be attributed only to an abstraction: only 'an event of the *kind* E' may be said to be regularly accompanied by 'events of the kinds C_1 C_2 etc.' which, by invoking a general law, may be recognized as its causal conditions.

Thus an 'historical' enquiry cast in the form of a causal explanation of the occurrence of an 'event' of a certain kind may be expected to run somewhat as follows:

> Here, first, is a statement, 'reasonably well confirmed by empirical evidence', reporting that an Act of Parliament was enacted (occurred) on such and such date. Do not go to the Statute Book, seek to discover the concern of this Act or how this concern came to be formulated in a Bill laid before Parliament; our business is solely with the occurrence of an 'Event' of a specified *kind*, namely, any parliamentary enactment. Here, secondly, are a number of statements (similarly confirmed) reporting and asserting the occurrence of other 'events' of certain kinds; namely, parliamentary debates (*what* was said is of no interest to this historian), readings of the Bill, committee stages, reports, consents, votes, assents etc. etc. which preceded and accompanied this 'Event', worthy of attention here because they alone are of the kind which must regularly (that is, are required by universal laws) accompany an event of this kind. These universal laws (in this case rules of a required procedure) identify the necessary precedents and accompaniments of the occurrence of an 'Event' of this kind, and consequently may be recognized as the causal conditions of its occurrence. Thus, a statement reporting the occurrence of an 'Event' of a certain kind has been transformed into the conclusion of a deductive argument. *QED*.

But neither in the procedure it follows nor the conclusions it seeks is it recognizable as even a parody of historical enquiry and understanding.

8

An historical enquiry recognized as an engagement to infer, from a present of authenticated survivals, a past which has not survived and to understand the character of the not yet understood events which compose this past as the outcomes of antecedent events to which they are significantly related, leaves unspecified the character to be attributed to this relationship. But those who purport to argue that, in order to be significant, it must be a causal relationship in fact do nothing of the kind. Instead, they direct our attention to an entirely different sort of enquiry; namely, an enquiry designed to deduce the occurrence of an already specified kind of 'event' alleged to have happened by relating it to the occurrence of already specified antecedent events, also alleged to have happened, this relationship being recognized to be causal in virtue of a universal law which declares that these kinds of antecedents invariably precede the kind of event whose occurrence is to be deduced. And to be concerned with this kind of enquiry is to have resigned any pretence of being concerned with the conditions of historical understanding.

Nevertheless, the word 'cause' is a commonplace expression of historical discourse and we may perhaps discern something of its meaning there by considering the occasions of its customary use and the conditions to which it is apt to refer. When in a summary account of the past, a list of events antecedent to an alleged event ('the French Revolution' or 'the Thirty Years' War') is said to be a list of its 'causes' the statement is ambiguous until the alleged effect is more closely specified, and the word 'cause' is clearly insignificant; a rhetorical expression meaning no more than 'noteworthy antecedents'. Nothing is said to warrant or even to suggest the attribution of a causal status to this brief selection of diverse circumstances antecedent to an event of which, as yet, we have been told nothing except a name. And no general 'law' is invoked.

Further, the word 'cause' is commonly employed in

historical writing in respect of assignable actions in an enquiry to relate them to their alleged outcomes. Here, a causal status is often attributed to an action if, in performing it, the agent may be supposed to have 'intended' the outcome, which thereby is recognized to be a consequence. But if such an enquiry is to reach an intelligible conclusion arbitrary limits must be set both upon the considerations in terms of which intentionality is recognized and upon what shall count as the outcome of an action. Must we look for evidence of a deliberated plan and of foresight in detail of what may ensue, or may we recognize intention in terms of commonsense expectations, or will something less than this be enough? And to what distance are we to take the reverberating outcomes of an action when it is qualified by the responses it receives in order that they may be recognized as its consequences? But when these considerations are taken into account, the enquiry reveals itself, not as a concern with a relationship of cause and effect, but as an engagement to establish responsibility (or perhaps blame); and not as an historical enquiry concerned, for example, to understand the character of the so-called Massacre of St Bartholomew's Day as an *eventus*, but as a moral or judicial enquiry concerned to determine (within some practical rules of evidence) *who* may be held responsible for it. This resort to the language of causality itself announces a departure from the concerns of an historical enquiry: happenings understood not as events in terms of antecedent events but as the outcomes of the so-called intentions of assignable actions.

Or a causal status is sometimes attributed to an action not because its outcome may be attributed to the intention of its performer but in virtue of its being recognized to lie outside what is regarded as a settled state of affairs. But here again, such settled states of affairs belong to a practical understanding which is concerned with the mediation of continuous change and is disposed to seek an understanding of alleged novelties in their antecedents. And the attribution of a causal status to such intrusive 'pushes' generating change belongs to the rhetoric of persuasion rather than the logic of historical enquiry.

In short, the word 'cause' in historical discourse is commonly a loose, insignificant expression employed, for the most part, either to emphasize an alleged circumstantially noteworthy condition, or when the enquiry is abridged to a concern to determine the 'responsibility' of agents for the outcomes (or the foreshortened outcomes) of their alleged actions, or to underline a reputed abnormality. But what is perhaps more to the point, when the word purports (as it may) to stand for a significant relationship between antecedent events and a subsequent historical event[27] all that properly (or even distantly) belongs to the notion of causality is necessarily denied or excluded.

An historian, concerned to understand the character of an historical event in terms of its significant relationship to antecedent events and disposed to use the word 'cause' to denote this relationship, does not and cannot claim to be invoking any of the Aristotelian 'causes' or the conceptions of causality argued by philosophers (like Leibnitz) who have considered the matter: these are not relationships between events separated by an interval of time. Nor is the relationship between events denoted in an historian's use of the word 'cause' either necessary, sufficient or exclusive: he is not suggesting that the formula of historical understanding is, 'Whenever *A*, then *B* and only *B*.' And the notions, either that the word 'cause' here may stand for 'causal factors' which are not themselves historical events, or that this relationship between events may be expressed in terms of a 'law', are both excluded: it must stand for a relationship between events, and an historian is not concerned with events merely in terms of their kinds or merely to explain the occurrence of an alleged kind of consequent. Since he is not concerned with 'origins', the word cannot signify some 'originating' or 'abnormal' event. And since he is concerned to distinguish between signi-

[27] Even Ranke, on occasion, writes of the significant *Zusammenhang* between historical events as a *Causalnexus*.

ficant and insignificant antecedents, the word cannot stand for the total of all antecedents;[28] nor may it stand for one such antecedent on the ground that had it not occurred the occurrence of the subsequent would be a logical impossibility.[29] Nor again, is the task attributed to historical enquiry that of 'marshalling events in a chain of causes and effects': the antecedents which may be said to be the 'causal' conditions of a subsequent are not necessarily themselves causally related to one another. And lastly, since it is recognized that an historical event is a manifold identity with multiple and divergent relationships with a variety of subsequents, historical enquiry cannot be concerned with the question, What did this event, or these events, cause? but only with their non-exclusive relationship with some subsequent event in terms of which the character of that subsequent may be understood.[30]

[28] Cf. J. S. Mill, 'The real cause is the whole of these antecedents and we have, philosophically speaking, no right to give the name of cause to any one exclusive of the others' (*A System of Logic*, III, V, §3).

[29] E.g. the birth of Julius Caesar recognized as a causal condition of his crossing the Rubicon.

[30] After an ambiguous and confused debate extending over nearly two centuries, a belief in Purgatory, which as late as the early decades of the sixteenth century had remained highly important, had become inconspicuous in popular belief and theological writing in England by the middle of the seventeenth century. In seeking to transform this alleged happening into an historical event (that is, to understand its historical character) a significant relationship has been conjectured between it and the Acts of 1545 and 1547 abolishing the Chantries, which were the chief among the endowed foundations concerned with intercession for souls in Purgatory. It has been said that these Acts were 'the most shattering and irreversible actions of the Reformation in England'. Now, an historian who identified this relationship as a causal *nexus* is perhaps treading dangerous ground but at least it is clear what he is *not* affirming.

He is certainly not saying that the abolition of the Chantries was the necessary and sufficient cause of the desuetude of the

These are not arbitrary qualifications of the notion of causality. They relate to the character of an historical enquiry. They represent the assumption that historical

---

belief. And the so-called 'causal' relationship he is pointing to (with a somewhat shaky finger) is not derived from the assumption of some such definitive or statistical regularity as 'when one of the most common expressions of a belief is extinguished the belief cannot survive'. What he is suggesting requires no such postulate which, incidentally, assumes that which he is seeking to understand to be already understood. Consequently, he may be said to be using the word 'cause' somewhat loosely.

But further, in affirming this so-called 'causal' relationship he is not suggesting that the antecedent 'determined' the occurrence of the subsequent, because what he is seeking is an understanding of the subsequent and not to account for the occurrence of an already understood subsequent. And he cannot mean that he has evidence to show that the antecedent 'determined' the character of the subsequent because such evidence would be discernible only if he already understood the character of the subsequent. Nor is he merely pointing to a conceptual resemblance between the antecedent and the subsequent. He knows well enough that such a resemblance does not preclude significant historical relationship, but he knows also that it does not itself constitute such a relationship and is not a necessary condition of such a relationship. Indeed, to identify an antecedent and a subsequent in terms of conceptual affinity is to transform them into analytic components of an already understood situation and to deprive them of their characters as historical events. Nor is he referring to the beliefs of those concerned about how they came to resign their belief in Purgatory: he does not mean that those who ceased to believe attributed this change to the abolition of the Chantries. And of course he is not saying anything about the intentions of the Acts of 1545 and 1547: he does not mean that these Acts were expressly designed to undercut the belief in Purgatory and that they achieved their purpose, or that (if this were found to be, in part or in whole, their design) it would identify them as causal conditions of the situation he has provisionally identified as the desuetude of the belief. What he may (and what he usually does) mean remains to be considered.

enquiry is concerned with relationships between events and that cause and effect here are separated by an interval of time. They presuppose, not that each historical event is unique, but that the business of historical enquiry is with events in respect of their individuality, not merely in place and time, but of character. And they presume that this exploration of the antecedents of an event is concerned, not merely to account for its occurrence, but to understand its character.

But these qualifications and reservations in respect of causality are fatal to any serious claim of such an historical enquiry to be concerned with causal relationships. What is here spoken of as a 'causal' (and therefore a significant) relationship between historical events cannot be recognized as a causal relationship properly speaking. The word 'cause', when it appears in historical discourse as a relationship between historical events, is a misnomer. Nevertheless, it would, I think, be absurd to suggest that the word 'cause' be excised from the vocabulary of historical discourse. When it appears there it should be allowed to be (what it already means in most respectable historical writing) no more than an expression of the concern of an historical enquiry to seek significant relationships between historical events and to distinguish between those antecedent conditions which are significant for the understanding of a subsequent and those that are not. And we should, and shall, look elsewhere for a specification (and a more appropriate name) for the relationship actually being sought and employed when in historical discourse the word 'cause' is invoked.

Meanwhile, notice may be taken of some less comprehensive, but not less defective, characterizations of the significant relationship between historical events sought in an historical enquiry and the procedures in which it may be established: namely, the contention that the undertaking to anatomize an historical situation may be promoted (or even satisfied) by comparing it with other allegedly similar situations, and the parallel contention that the relationship between an historical event and its significant antecedents is one of conceptual similarity or even identity; the view that a passage of significantly related historical events may be composed of a 'correlation' of occurrences; and the notion that it may be composed in terms of analogical relationships. Here, as in the case of an engagement to establish causal relationships, historical events are reduced to examples of kinds of occurrences, and a search for mutual relationships is substituted for those between antecedents and subsequents.

It would be absurd to contend that an enquiry designed to identify and anatomize the character of an historical situation may not be advanced by comparing it with other situations related to it solely in respect of their alleged similarity. Nevertheless, the conditions of this procedure are severe and its product small. The comparison must be in respect of detail; nothing can come of the observation of merely general or superficial resemblances.[31] The situations compared in respect of their similarity must be otherwise unrelated. That which is adduced for comparison must be better understood than the situation being anatomized. And what is being sought in comparison (an historical situation more perspicuously anatomized) is at best a possible by-product of the procedure of such comparison and in no sense a conclusion. But with these conditions satisfied and its ambiguity recognized (similarities recognized before their terms have been explored), 'comparison' and the recognition of similarities may be regarded as a heuristic device valuable for the hypotheses it may suggest.

[31] The resemblance between Lutheran doctrine and the Mahayanaian Buddhist belief in the possibility of salvation by faith in the power of the bodhisattva Amitabha to bring his devotees, after death, to the Pure Land of Paradise has been found interesting, but it is difficult to imagine how an observation of it might promote a more exact analysis of Lutheran doctrine. And the identification of two or more situations merely as 'revolutionary' is historically insignificant.

But to recognize comparison as a valuable heuristic device in an enquiry designed to anatomize an historical situation is not to give it a place in the logic of historical enquiry. For where the engagement is not to anatomize a situation but to translate it into a conjunction of significantly related events and to understand its character in terms of its antecedents, the observation of conceptual similarities between antecedents and a subsequent becomes merely a distracting irrelevance. And this is not because such likenesses may not be observed, but because conceptual likenesses or identities cannot themselves constitute significant relationships between historical events and where such relationships are observed such similarities are of no account whatsoever. A passage of historically related events is the product of inference, but it does not itself compose an argument.

Secondly, there is the contention that an historical past may be composed of what is called a 'correlation' of events. A correlation is a mutual relationship in terms of which dissimilars are observed to be linked in a certain (usually measurable) respect without there being any recognizable reason for this connection. And the detection and exploration of correlations is a device for composing situations or for specifying already identified situations in terms of proportionate relationships between their otherwise dissimilar features. The mutual relationship may be close (what is called a 'high' correlation), or it may be not so close; but a correlation may be any proportional relationship or any steady variation in a proportional relationship. Thus it has been observed that in a sample of British schoolboys aged 16, there was a close correlation between their height and the figure they scored in an intelligence test; and it might be observed that the yearly number of births in a certain Tyrolean village was, over a stated period of time, exactly half the number of storks inhabiting the rooftops. As such, a correlation means no more than what it announces: namely, that there is an observed but unexplained mutual relationship between certain, usually quantified, abstractions. It may be dismissed as a mere coincidence; that is, nothing more than a correlation. Or it may be used pragmatically to estimate or to forecast other similar situations elsewhere or at another time. Or it may be made the subject of further research, designed, if possible, to deprive it of its character as a mere correlation by finding for it a reason or a cause and thus transforming it into a significant relationship. Thus, H. T. Buckle, observing a correlation between the number of marriages in a parish and the price of corn, had no difficulty in transforming it into a significant relationship in terms of the cost of maintaining a household, although this would not take account of a year in which the price of corn rose and the number of unmarried men or women of marriageable age in the parish was abnormally low. But by itself a correlation has the insignificance of a merely external relationship.

However, if procedures of sampling were renounced and if inference from record permitted it, it would seem by no means impossible, in an enquiry to anatomize an historical situation, to abstract quantified features from it and, if they were sufficiently numerous and were plotted on a graph, to display the situation as a structure composed of correlations. Indeed, this adventure in so-called cliometrics has been attempted. But whatever its virtues, it is not to be expected that such a representation of an historical situation would itself satisfy an historian concerned to understand it in terms of the significant relationships of its component occurrences. It would provide him with no answers, although it might suggest interesting questions to pursue. And where the enquiry is concerned with events and with understanding their characters in terms of their antecedents, the observation of correlations can have no place at all. Historical events are not themselves reducible to examples of kinds of occurrences, antecedents and subsequents cannot be *mutually* related, and what they are may be discerned only in terms of their significant sequential relationship.

Lastly, there is analogical relationship to be considered.

To perceive or to acknowledge an analogy is to allege a relationship in terms of functional similarity between certain attributes of objects or occurrences otherwise unlike one another. What is asserted in alleging an analogical relationship is neither an observable, nor a direct, nor a complete resemblance but only a symbolic correspondence of attributes. Thus a king may be spoken of as 'the shepherd of his people', the House of Commons as an assembly of representatives of shareholders in a corporation, music as 'the food of love', an evangelist as a fisherman, and a man as a marigold. Analogies may be more or less apt, they may be multiplied, they may be extended and elaborated in allegory, and they belong both to the logic of persuasion and obliquely to the logic of practical understanding. But analogical relationship may have no place in the logic of historical understanding. Indeed, a past composed in terms of such relationships is not an historical past composed of related events but a practical past composed of parables, emblematic happenings and exemplars of human conduct.

9

I have argued that an historical past is a past that has not, and could not have, survived but is a past inferred from a present–past of survivals and is the conclusion of an historical enquiry. And further, I have distinguished it as a past composed of historical events. By an historical event I mean a past happening or situation which has not survived understood in terms of the antecedent happenings and situations, similarly understood, to which it is significantly related. Thus, an historical event is itself a convergence of significantly related historical events. And an historical enquiry is an engagement to infer and to assemble a passage of related historical events as itself an answer to an historical question about the past. Its design is to compose and to understand the characters of historical events by

assembling the passages of related events which constitute their characters. It cannot be a concern merely to
account for the occurrence of an already understood event
because an historical event is not a happening or a situation
which occurred or could have occurred,[32] and its character
cannot be understood in advance of an historical enquiry.
On this view of the matter the question to be considered is:
What is the relationship between antecedent historical
events and a subsequent historical event in terms of which
they may be understood to compose the passage of events
which converge to constitute the character of the subsequent?

In considering this question I have argued that the
relationship cannot be a fortuitous relationship: chance is
the exemplar of purely external, insignificant relationship.
And I have argued that it cannot be a genuinely causal
relationship. I have perhaps given excessive attention to
the claim that it must be of this character, but that is because
the word 'cause' has a secure place in the vocabulary of
historical discourse and also because causality is expressly
invoked in many current accounts of the logic of historical
understanding. But I have not had to argue the fundamental incoherence of the idea of a causal *nexus* because
its claim in respect of historical understanding may be
disposed of more frugally. I have noticed some other
manifestly inadequate specifications of this relationship.
And further, it should perhaps be repeated that since an
historical event is not an assignable action, the antecedents
in terms of which its character may come to be understood
cannot be an agent's reasons, intentions, motives or
deliberative calculations. What I am seeking is, then, the
kind of relationship which, when in an historical enquiry it
is found to subsist between antecedent events and a
subsequent event, composes an identity which may be
described, alternatively, as an event properly understood

[32] In the sense of being observed to be happening or of being
recognized to have happened.

as an outcome of antecedent events, or as an assemblage of events related in such a manner as itself to constitute an historically understood event. I shall call it a contingent relationship.

The word 'contingent' (or, more properly, 'contingentially'), like the words 'causally', 'functionally', 'probably' and so on, stands for a relationship. Historical events are not themselves contingent, they are related to one another contingently. This kind of relationship is, first, one of proximity and of 'touch'; an immediate relationship. An historical past, composed conceptually of contiguous historical events has no place for extrinsic general terms of relationship – the glue of normality or the cement of general causes. When an historian assembles a passage of antecedent events to compose a subsequent he builds what in the countryside is called a 'dry wall': the stones (that is, the antecedent events) which compose the wall (that is, the subsequent event) are joined and held together, not by mortar, but in terms of their shapes. And the wall, here, has no premeditated design; it is what its components, in touching, constitute.

Secondly, it is a circumstantial relationship; not in terms of similarity, of kind, of family resemblance, of conceptual affinity, mutuality, design, causality, probability and so on, but a relationship of evidential contiguity. Of course similarities of character between antecedent and subsequent events may be discernible, but they do not themselves constitute historically significant relationships.

Thirdly, an enquiry designed to assemble a passage of antecedent events in terms of which to compose and to understand a subsequent is concerned to distinguish among these contiguous antecedents those which may be recognized to be significantly related to it because, in touching, they impart not themselves but a difference, to discern the difference they made, and thus to characterize the subsequent as a circumstantial confluence of antecedent historical events. Nevertheless, this contingent relationship between antecedents and a subsequent, in terms of which the character of the subsequent comes to be understood as a kind of consequent, is not an exclusive relationship. These antecedents are not absorbed in this subsequent but remain eligible to be significantly related to a variety of other subsequents. And it is my contention that when an historical writer uses the word 'cause' what he implicitly refers to is this contingent, circumstantial relationship of antecedent events to a subsequent whose differences converge to compose the difference which constitutes the character of the subsequent.

An historical event, then, has no necessary or essential character. It is a conflation of accessories which, here, have no exclusive characters but are the difference they made in a convergence of differences which compose a circumstantial historical identity. Such identities may differ in magnitude and in complexity, but they are alike in being the conclusions of enquiries and themselves answers to historical questions about the past which admit of no other kind of answer. An historical enquiry is not an explanatory exercise, nor is it a concern to solve a problem; it is an engagement to infer, to understand discursively and to imagine the character of an historical event. It begins in a present–past of survivals, and at each stage it is necessarily sustained only in terms of a reading of the circumstantial evidence it invokes. To seek the authentic utterance of a survival from the past, to anatomize a situation which has not survived, and to understand the character of an historical event which could not have survived, each are enquiries concerned to understand what has been somehow identified but the character of which is not yet understood. An historian is never in a position to look back from an already understood historical situation or event and to conclude what must have been its components or significant antecedents. And the conclusion of an historical enquiry cannot be confirmed or falsified by comparing it with the conclusions of any other kind of enquiry, and it cannot be tested against independent criteria of credibility – those of a current common sense or of a reading of so-called 'human nature'. As nothing here is necessary, so also nothing is impossible. Historical writings differ greatly in the perceptiveness they exhibit in the consideration of the circumstantial evidence they employ, in the quality of the imagination they display in the construction of an historical event, and in the idiosyncratic deviations of their authors from this engagement, but somewhere in every genuine historical enquiry there is an undertaking of this sort, and this is what constitutes it an historical enquiry.

III   Historical Change

Identity and continuity

1

As a mode of enquiry and understanding history is, of course, abstract and conditional, and it may itself be understood in terms of its conditions. I have considered two of these: the idea of an historical past and the idea of an historical event which included a consideration of the relationship that subsists between historical events in terms of which they may be made to compose assemblages of events significantly related to outcomes, themselves historical events. These conditions distinguish history from all other engagements to understand the past, particularly a practical understanding of the past, which it excludes but does not deny.[1] I shall now consider a third postulate of historical understanding: the idea of historical change.

[1] When Milton's Manoah exhorted the Messenger bearing the news of Samson's death to 'Tell us the sum, the circumstance defer' (*Samson Agonistes*, l. 1557) he recognized 'history' but declared his wish not at the moment to be bothered with it, wanting only to learn of the situation to which an immediate response was called for. But no doubt he only dimly perceived that this 'sum' when related to antecedent circumstances and transformed into an historical event would turn out to be of a categorially different character from that of the Messenger's report.

In going beyond the engagement to anatomize an alleged immobile past situation in terms of its related component occurrences and in undertaking the transformation of such a situation into an historical event by understanding it as the outcome of an assembled passage of antecedent events significantly related to it, an historical enquiry invokes an idea of change. Antecedent events are recognized as differences, each understood in terms of the difference it made in an assembled confluence of differences which comprise the conditions of the coming into being of a subsequent and which converge to constitute its historical character. And such differences may be recognized as a significant passage of differences only in terms of an idea of change. Our question is, then, what exact and distinctive meaning may be attributed to the expression 'historical change'? And since my answer to this question is implicit in what I have already said about significant relationship between historical events, I propose to argue the matter here in a somewhat different style.

2

Change is a paradoxical idea. It is the notion of alteration combined with the notion of remaining the same. If there were no alteration there would be an unbroken sameness; if there were no remaining the same there would be the recollection of that which had unaccountably gone and the observation of that which had unaccountably appeared. We recognize the diurnal happening as change only because we take the sun that rose this morning to be the same sun as that which set last evening. The idea of change is a holding together of two apparently opposed but in fact complementary ideas: that of alteration and that of sameness; that of difference and that of identity.

Our most familiar notion of change is that in which differences are attributed to something which itself remains unaltered; that is, the identity required for difference to be recognizable as change is that which in the situation remains unaltered.

If I shuffle a pack of cards, the pack (the number and the kinds of cards) remains unaltered; what is different is the order of the cards in the pack. And it is because there is this unaltered identity combined with difference that shuffling is recognizable as change. If I ask for change for a pound note I shall expect to be given coins whose value is the same as that of a pound note. The unaltered identity is the value, the difference is the number and kinds of the tokens that add up to this value. This is the mode of change signified in the announcement that in future the 6.15 to Brighton will leave from platform 6 instead of from platform 8: the same train but a different place of departure. Change here is a difference of place, time, use, order, colour, size and so on, attributed to an unaltered identity.

Now, in an historical enquiry which seeks to understand the not yet understood character of an historical event as the outcome of an assemblage of antecedent events significantly related to it, these antecedents are being understood to compose a passage of differences from which this subsequent emerged. But this passage of differences, which includes its outcome, cannot be understood as a passage of change in terms of a notion of change in which difference is recognizable as change because it is attributed to an unaltered item in the situation. A past composed entirely of historical events and their relations is a past composed entirely of differences: it is a past from which such an unchanged identity has been expressly excluded. This does not mean that the components of an historically understood past are incessantly changing; nor does it require that no recognition be given to relative durabilities. It means only that the notion of historical change is not that of difference attributed to some changeless item in the situation. And if some plausibility attaches to the claim that an historical past may be understood in terms of this notion of change, it derives from the way in which some historical enquiries are described and from the titles they are given, and not from how the enquiries are themselves conducted.

We may be offered 'A History of Parliament' and it might appear that we are to be given an account of the changing fortunes of an institution situated in the Palace of Westminster, composed of appointed or elected persons and devoted to an unchanging function. But such expectations will be quickly dissipated. We find instead that each of these purported identities (of place, constitution and function) and any others that might be suggested, are themselves differences and that the history is composed in terms of some other notion of change. We may be offered 'A History of France', but only if its author has abandoned the engagement of an historian in favour of that of an ideologue or a mythologist shall we find in it an identity – *La Nation* or *La France* – to which the differences that compose the story are attributed. Or consider a biography. It may announce itself as 'the life and times' of John Smith, but the biographer will not (unless he is the victim of a theory) present it as the fortunes of its subject, its subject being an unaltered John Smith from birth to death. Indeed, he will know it to be his business to display John Smith himself as a continuity of differences and be puzzled to put his finger upon the identity he is using to do so. The formal identity of a name will not serve his purpose, nor will John Smith's gene structure or his soul.

The expression 'A History of English Agriculture', on the other hand, may seem a more promising subject to be understood in terms of this mode of change. The unchanging identity might be supposed to be the earth of England regarded as a capital resource and the 'history' to be an account of the changing manners in which this unchanging resource has been exploited: the crops which at different times it has to be made to grow, the changing methods of cultivation, the alteration in the shapes and sizes of the fields and so on. But the promise soon evaporates. This so-called 'earth' of England has not remained unchanged and it is historically inconceivable that it should have done so: it has altered in area, in conformation, in chemical composition and so on. The draining of the Fens was a gross addition to this capital resource; the erosion of the sea and the use of land for other than agricultural purposes has been a continuous diminution. Even here, from the historian's point of view, there is no item in the situation which is not itself a difference.

Of course, it is not impossible to find historians who seem to regard historical understanding as an account of change in which differences are attributed to fixed identities. What Lovejoy calls a 'unit idea' is an alleged changeless identity and its 'history' is an account of its movements about the world, the various uses to which it has been put and the different contexts in which it has appeared: the changing fortunes of an identity that never changes its value, is never coloured by the company it keeps, suffers no wear and tear, but from time to time may 'migrate' to a different place, may go underground, disappear from human discourse, perhaps later to be recollected and recalled for use, perhaps lost beyond recall. But neither here, nor (for example) in the enquiries of those who have explored the history of European political discourse in terms of the more durable vocabularies (linguistic conventions and general ideas) it has employed to express its various and less durable purposes, is it suggested that historical change is eligible to be understood as differences related to a genuinely changeless component. Such vocabularies may be long-lived, but for an historian they must be historical eventualities and, having emerged, they are themselves passages of change. In short, where an historical past is understood to be composed of historical events (that is, differences) assembled in answer to an historical question there is no room for an identity which is not itself a difference.

3

But this, which may perhaps be called a 'practical' mode, is not the only mode of change, and I shall consider next teleological change and the eligibility of historical change to be understood in terms of teleology.

The idea of teleological change is that of a succession of differences which may be recognized as change because each is recognized as an indispensable step or stage in a process in which a potential becomes an actual. It is a process of change in which X, in a sequence of transformations, becomes Y and in which Y is understood to have been potential in X. This is a genuine conception of change: there is difference and there is identity. But instead of the identity being a separable item in the situation (like the pack of cards when it is shuffled) it is an unchanging purpose or destiny which is present from the beginning, which determines the differences and their sequential succession, and which is achieved when the process of change is completed.

The notion that 'the past' constitutes a single teleological process, which a masterful historian may be expected to exhibit in its entirety (at least in outline) and of which one less ambitious may engage to elucidate some selected passage, is absurd. One might, like Kant, imagine the human race to be embarked upon such a purposeful journey, but an historical enquiry here must at least be an undertaking to expose its teleology and this is inherently impossible while the historian remains ignorant (as he must be) both of its beginning and its end. Augustine, for example, could represent the history of the world from the Creation (or perhaps from the expulsion from Eden) to the coming of Christ as a unique passage of change in the teleological mode only because he had identified its initial condition and its end, could argue that this end was a genine conclusion potential in this beginning and could therefore interpret the intervening events as necessary steps on the way to this conclusion. But, even so, he recognized this to be a 'prophetic' (not an historical) interpretation of this particular passage of the past, taking account of only a selection of the more 'important' happenings, and to be impossible to discern in respect of any subsequent, yet incomplete, passage of the past.

Consequently, the contention that historical change may be identified with teleological change is not even plausible unless the historical past is understood to be composed of a number of completed (but teleologically unrelated) teleological processes, either comprehensive completed chapters of human experience (like Spengler's 'cultures' or Toynbee's 'civilizations') or segments of conceptually identified human engagements, like Trotsky's 'economic régimes'.[2] But even when we ignore the perverse notion of historical enquiry as an engagement to understand reported occurrences in terms of the place they occupy in some exclusive teleological process and to reject as non-events those that cannot be assigned such a place, I do not think this claim in respect of historical change can be sustained.

First, a teleological process is recognizable as a passage of change in virtue of the differences which compose it being understood as exemplary stages which succeed one another in a uniform order and in which an initial condition, identified in terms of its kind, reaches an exemplary *terminus* already known to be potential in it. Thus a kettle of water coming to the boil may be represented as a passage of teleological change. Here, the initial condition is a measurable source of heat and water with a known and limited capacity for absorbing heat. The differences which compose this passage of change are readings on a thermometer; a uniform succession of stages which succeed one another until the water has absorbed all the heat it is capable of absorbing and the thermometer, at sea level, reads 212° on the Fahrenheit scale. But the differences that compose a passage of historical change are not exemplary stages

[2] Whether such a passage of the past is represented as the inevitable working-out of the self-contradictions of its initial condition, leading to its final collapse, or is composed of steps leading to a final positive achievement, is merely a distinction within the notion of teleological change.

which, impelled by a potentiality, succeed one another to issue in a *terminus* which is not itself a difference. They are an assemblage of multiform, unrelated historical events, gathered from here and there, the alleged antecedents of an outcome, itself a difference, whose unknown and unforeseeable character they circumstantially converge to compose.

Secondly, a teleology is an ideal process of change which, protected by the terms of its abstraction, is incapable either of diverging from its course or of failing to reach its destination. Acorns are potential oak trees and in a sequence of exemplary differences they are set to reach their inherent *terminus* and no other. And with the recognition of oak trees as the sole producers of acorns this process may be represented as one of cyclical teleological change. No oak without an antecedent acorn; no acorn without a potential oak. But when, as in a historical enquiry, we quit this world of abstraction and attend to *was eigentlich geschehen ist* we are obliged to recognize that this or that acorn may be baulked of its teleological destiny: it may be eaten by a hog. But this does not mean that an historian must be prepared, like Aristotle, to qualify teleological change by the admission of an ingredient of 'accident', or, like Burke, disposed to think of the human past as a divinely designed teleological order, be ready, in recognition of human waywardness, to conclude that this order could prevail only in the long run and then only if it included a device for the periodic and circumstantial correction of the deviations due to human errancy.[3] Nor does it mean that an historian should be prepared, on occasion, to abandon the notion of teleological change. It means than an historical past may *never* be cast in the mode of teleological change. 'No oak trees without acorns' may be a formally true

[3] Historians who have seriously embraced the notion of teleological change have sometimes sought to make it a more plausible model for historical change by excluding from it certain considerations (such as 'the time it takes'), or by building into it some *ad hoc* principle of 'accident', such as Trotsky's 'law of

proposition, but that this acorn did in fact produce this oak tree, there and then, is not a teleological necessity; it is a circumstantial occurrence which has no place whatever in a process of teleological change. And conversely, an historian concerned to understand the coming into being of a certain forest of oaks in terms of its historical antecedents will not begin with the observation that there must have been a lot of acorns about (any more than an historical biographer of the Duke of Wellington will begin with the observation that he must have had a human mother and father); he will seek to relate it to antecedent historical events, such as that this forest of oaks was planted in 1720 by Capability Brown when he was landscaping the grounds of the newly built Blenheim.

Nevertheless, historical enquiry and understanding have sometimes affected the language of teleological change. We may put on one side the claim that 'the history of the world' may be understood as a teleological process, and also the contention that the past is a 'history-less' void except where it has been reduced to a number of necessarily unrelated passages of teleological change. But where a passage of historical change is said to be a 'dialectical' process, where it is spoken of as 'development' and when it is represented as 'progressive'[4] or 'purposive', teleology (or something akin to it) is being invoked. On most such occasions, however, this is no more than a somewhat inadvertent nod in the direction of teleological change, purporting, perhaps, to distinguish historical change from a merely fortuitous succession of happenings and, regard-

---

unevenness', designed to account for such deviations from teleological rectitude as an 'economic régime' collapsing 'before it has exhausted all its possibilities' (*History of the Russian Revolution*, I, pp. 23, 52; II, p. 220).

[4] What I refer to here is not a 'belief in progress' (that is, an understanding of the practical past, present and future), but the assimilation of the concept of historical change to that of progressive change.

less of what is appropriate, doing so in terms that will do this most effectively.[5] Or it may be no more than an insignificant surrender to fashionable analogy.[6] Or it may be recognized as a fumbling attempt to endow historical understanding with a 'philosophical' character it cannot sustain. And the so-called 'Whig' historians (concerned with the emergence of 'the British Constitution') and their counterparts elsewhere, sought to construct a practical past in terms of teleological change in order to give its outcome the supposedly superior status of a 'natural', an inevitable or an admirable character.[7] But in order to retain the teleological integrity of their story they were obliged to ignore, as non-events, many of the vicissitudes of the historical story. In short, teleological history is, in principle, a self-contradiction, and where it has been attempted it is usually a self-confessed botch.

4

A third mode of change offers itself for consideration as a model in terms of which to understand historical change: I will call it, for want of a better word, 'organic' change. Here, the identity required for the recognition of change is neither a distinguishable item in the situation immune from change, nor is it a kind of potency to be actualized. The unchanging identity in organic change is a 'law' or normal-

[5] 'The history of a literary *genre* is not the enumeration of the writers who have cultivated it. . . . The *genre* is regarded as an organism which contains within itself possibilities of development, and the history must show how far and in what way these possibilities have been realized' (E. K. Bennett, *A History of the German Novelle*).

[6] The use of the expression 'The Development of . . .' in place of 'A History of . . .' in the titles of historical works which nevertheless display nothing recognizable as 'development'.

[7] H. Butterfield, *The Whig Interpretation of History*.

ity which specifies the general character of the differences and perhaps the order of their occurrence.

One form of organic change, namely *homeostasis*, need not detain us long: it has little to offer as a model in terms of which to understand historical change. Here, change is a process of organic self-maintenance. A sea-anemone, for example, is wholly reconstituted from year to year, no cell remaining unchanged, in a continuous series of differences each of which is interpreted as a movement of self-maintenance. Change, here, is total change. And there is no teleology, no potentiality becoming actual. The identity is the law of change which may be formulated in a general law of self-maintenance (reluctance to perish), or it may be broken down into the normalities of a biochemical process sometimes called *metastasis*.

As a model for historical change, *homeostasis* is unpromising. Historical enquiry may acquaint us with a relatively immobile situation anatomized in terms of its tensions: the situation of the English gentry in the seventeenth century, the Scottish Enlightenment, the *entente cordiale* of 1904, Calvinist Geneva in the mid-sixteenth century. But there is no warrant for imposing the character of an organism upon such a situation and for understanding the continuous gyrations of its tensions as movements of self-maintenance, as if the only alternative were to be or not to be. To do so merely assigns a single general character to all such situations and their component differences and not only ignores the circumstantial conditions of these differences but also stands in the way of an historical enquiry in which the situation might be transformed into an historical event. If, for example, we were to identify England in the sixteenth century as an 'economy' and were to understand an 'economy' as an organism bent upon self-maintenance, and were to recognize one of its organic characteristics as a built-in resistance to having resources tied up in less than optimally productive enterprise, then (on certain assumptions about the diseconomy of monastic agriculture) we might recognize the dissolution of the monasteries in terms of the operation of a law of *homeostasis*. But whatever enlightenment we might suppose ourselves to have derived from this understanding of the dissolution it would certainly not be an historical enlightenment. Indeed, so far from providing a model in terms of which to identify historical change, the analogy (for it is no more) of *homeostasis* obstructs historical understanding by falsely purporting to make an historical enquiry unnecessary for reaching an historical conclusion.

There is, however, another form of organic change, sometimes called 'long-term *homeostasis*' but more commonly known as 'evolutionary' change, which (somewhat loosely understood) has more confidently been recognized as a model for historical change. Here, a succession of identifiable differences in the morphological or biological characteristics of a species of organism is recognized as a process of change in virtue of a 'law of development' which accounts for the general character and tendency of these differences and the order of their occurrence. The enquiries in which this understanding of organic change have been formulated and explored do not themselves suggest that it may have a universal application, but in the late nineteenth century it was often extended to cover the whole of human conduct[8] and it was identified by some as a notion of change supremely appropriate to historical enquiry and understanding. And indeed, in this respect it has some general features that make it seem not inappropriate. First,

[8] An anonymous writer in the late nineteenth century, quoted in W. D. P. Bliss, *The New Encyclopedia of Social Reform*, declared: 'The law of organic evolution does not stop with the development of the physical. It is the same throughout the entire realm of phenomena. It passes over into the immaterial and builds up political, social, and moral institutions in almost precisely the same manner as physical organisms are formed.' And Darwin's reference to the inspiration he had got from the writings of Malthus was quoted, by Benjamin Kidd (*Social Evolution*), as evidence that Darwin's conception of evolutionary change was partly derived from 'the observation of human society'.

it is a notion of change largely indifferent to 'how it all began', except that it excludes (especially in the case of the human species) a so-called 'original creation'. Secondly, change here is open-ended; there is no teleology and no suggestion that it may have a *finis ultimus* in a 'perfect' organism or of a cyclical succession of differences. And thirdly, the differences which compose an evolutionary process of change are identifiable modifications of the morphological or biological characteristics of an identifiable organic species, some perhaps discernible in fossil remains, which may not be forecast but which succeed one another in such a manner that *this* cannot have come before *that*: the counterpart of historical anachronism. Nevertheless, in spite of these affinities with historical change, there are I think two considerations which make impossible the understanding of an historical past in terms of evolutionary change: the impossibility of distinguishing in such a past an identity which even plausibly corresponds to an organic species, and the consequential impossibility of formulating an evolutionary law in terms of which to understand the differences which compose a passage of historical change, or even to account for their occurrence. They are two categorially different modes of change.

And these considerations are inevitably reflected in the historical writings which seek to employ the notion of evolutionary change. For although such writings some-times affect even the more recondite distinctions which belong to the notion of evolutionary change,[9] they confess that the expressions which properly belong to the vocabulary of evolution are no better than distant and inappropriate analogies when applied to historical change. An organic species identity is indiscriminately and implausibly attributed not only to 'civilizations', 'cultures', societies' (or even to 'society'), 'empires', 'bureaucracies' and so on, but

[9] A large or puzzling historical change, instead of being described in the language of drama as, perhaps, a 'revolution', is called a 'mutation', that is, a change which results in the production of a new species.

also to theologies, philosophical doctrines, literary *genres*, moralities, legal systems, architectural styles, to activities such as horse-racing and even to artefacts; thus depriving the expression of any distinct meaning.[10] And neither the occurrence nor the character of the differences with which these enquiries are concerned are ever, in fact, understood as examples of the operation of a law or laws of evolutionary change. Nor is the distinction between evolutionary change and historical change any less manifest where both are sustainable in respect of an ostensibly common concern. For example, vernaculars may perhaps be and certainly have been endowed with the character of organisms and at least some of the changes they display may be attributed to an *homeostatic* urge to retain or to improve their characters as expressive instruments of discourse, and some normalities of linguistic change may be discernible. But assuming this to be the case, the business of an historian lies elsewhere. He is concerned with some particular vernacular; and if this should be the English language he will be concerned with its differences understood as the outcomes of the linguistic encounters of Celts, Angles, Saxons, Danes, Normans etc., an assemblage of differences which cannot acquire an identity in terms of the idea of evolutionary change.

The word 'evolution', so long as it stands for a distinct mode of change, can have no proper place in the vocabulary of historical discourse; and it may survive there (as I have suggested the word 'cause' may survive) only if it is deprived of any exact meaning: as a fumbling, analogical expression for the slow-paced historical change exhibited in a large-scale historical enquiry, or simply to denote a

[10] Thus, *The Evolution of Parliament, The Evolution of the Novel, The Evolution of Law and Order, The Evolution of the Microscope, The Growth of English Representative Institutions, The Growth of Philosophical Radicalism, Civilization and the Growth of Law*, and such familiar expressions as 'the evolution of Prussia'. And 'war' (itself an alleged organism which evolves) is said to have 'done much to determine the evolution of mediaeval England'.

concern with *la longue durée* in which alleged historical changes are abridged to become examples of general tendencies.

There are, then, three well-articulated modes of change: change where the identity required for the recognition of change lies in an immutable item in the situation to which change is attributed, teleological change and organic change. Each offers itself as a model for historical change, but I have given my reasons for denying that historical change may be identified with any of them. And these reasons also exclude the attribution of an eclectic character to historical change in which an historical understanding may be sought and perhaps achieved by employing whichever of them may seem appropriate to the alleged character of the historical situation being explored.[11]

5

An historical past, the conclusion of an historical enquiry, is an assemblage of antecedent historical events (which may have no significant relationship to one another) in respect of what they contribute to the understanding of the

[11] There are, of course, many other inappropriate expressions employed in historical writings to denote change, but for the most part they are recognizable as informal versions of the modes of change I have noticed. Flowing and ebbing and waxing and waning are the attribution of differences to alleged unchanged identities and represent a practical rather than an historical understanding. And so also do the notions of rise, decline or fall, which often reflect ancient myth but are an expression of the practical observation that most interesting changes in human affairs are either 'up' or 'down' so far as the participants are concerned. The notion of change as 'growth' is ambiguous: it may (somewhat vaguely) represent a notion of *homeostasis*, but where it stands for change leading to a condition of 'maturity' it would seem to be teleological.

historical character of a subsequent event. And the question to be considered is, What mode of relationship must
subsist between these antecedents and a subsequent if its
historical character is to be discerned in their convergence?
Or, alternatively, since in an historical understanding each
antecedent historical event is a difference recognized, not
in terms of its substantive character, but in respect of the
difference it made in the differential character of a subsequent, an historical past may be recognized as a passage of
historical change. And here the question to be considered
is, What may constitute a distinguishable and a significant
passage of historical change? This question concerns the
identity (the sameness) in terms of which a passage of
differences may be recognized, not as a fortuitous succession of differences, but as itself a difference; that is, as a
passage of change. And an idea of historical change must
satisfy two conditions: that an historical past is composed
of nothing but historical events, and that every historical
event is a difference recognized in terms of the difference it
made in the constitution of the not yet understood character of a subsequent event, itself a difference. The identity
which constitutes a passage of historical change must be
itself a difference or a composition of differences, and every
such difference must be an historical event.

In an earlier essay I have argued that the relationship
between antecedent historical events and a subsequent
recognized as their outcome must be a contingent relationship. And I distinguished this from a relationship of
'chance', from a causal relationship and from a relationship
in terms of something called in from the outside, the glue of
normality or the cement of general causes. I shall now
argue that the identity in terms of which an assembled
passage of historical events, recognized as differences, may
be understood as a passage of change is nothing other than
its inherent continuity; this continuity to be distinguished
from some changeless item in the situation, from an
enduring purpose or end to be realized and from the
normalities or the 'law' of a process of change.

That the identity of a whole may be understood in terms of the continuity of its component parts was observed by Aristotle, who recognized continuity as a kind of contiguity.[12] This is the case, he alleged, whenever a whole is composed of distinguishable uniform parts which touch one another without interval and hold together in virtue of what they themselves are without extraneous mediation. Thus the identity, the oneness, of a length of chain composed of nothing but its links and serving no extraneous purpose lies in its continuity, which is itself a function of the contiguity of its parts. Whereas the identity of a chain whose links are held together by magnetic attraction, and which would fall to pieces if the current were cut off, lies elsewhere; and the identity of a chain attached to an anchor lies in its purpose.

But an historical enquiry is not concerned with the identity of a whole composed of uniform parts; it is concerned with the identity of an assembled passage of historical differences (events) in respect of their being the significant antecedents of a not yet understood subsequent historical difference (event). And this entails an idea of change; for a succession or an assemblage of differences may acquire an identity only by being understood in terms of change. But although an historical past is a passage of differences assembled to compose the character of an outcome, it cannot be recognized as a passage of change in virtue of its coming to compose this outcome because this outcome cannot be known in advance of its antecedents being assembled and it is not a *terminus* of another sort but, like its alleged antecedents, is itself only another difference. Further, since the passage of differences which composes an historical past is a passage of historical events devoid of fixed potentialities to issue in foregone conclusions, it cannot be given an identity, and recognized as a passage of change, in terms of a notion of teleological or dialectical

[12] *Physics*, V, 3, 277a: 'The continuous is a kind of contiguity. . . . It is found in things whose nature is such as to make them one when they are in contact.'

change or an idea of 'development'. And again, since these differences are actual historical events inferred from the circumstantial evidence supplied by surviving utterances and artefacts, and not kinds or classes of event, they cannot compose a passage of change in virtue of being recognized as examples of a 'law' of self-maintenance, an evolutionary 'law' or the product of some 'force' or 'factor' which is not itself an historical event. Certainly, such an assemblage of differences is understood to occupy time, but it cannot be given an identity and recognized as a passage of change in virtue of occupying a distinguishable period of time as distinct from a provenance composed of other events. And lastly, such a passage of antecedent differences related to a subsequent difference does not lie, already identified, somewhere in the past, waiting to be picked up; it does not exist until it is assembled by an historian in search of clues to the character of a not-yet-understood historical event.

In short, since what unites an assemblage of historical differences, gives it an identity and makes it recognizable as a passage of change cannot be something imposed upon it from the outside, we must seek it in some intrinsic quality of the assemblage itself, or else confess that an historical past is no more than a tissue of fortuitous conjunctions. And I suggest that this identity may be found in its own coherence; that is, in its character as a passage of differences which touch and modify one another and converge to compose a subsequent difference. But since this coherence is circumstantial, not conceptual, it may perhaps be more exactly understood as the continuity or the continuousness of the passages of differences; continuity being recognized as a kind of contiguity.[13] And an historical past may be

[13] The notion of change exemplified in Sir John Cutler's famous stockings has been thought to be that of historical change. These silk stockings were so continuously darned with wool that they became wholly transformed, not one particle of silk remaining. And it is suggested that in order to recognize what had happened as 'change' (and not a pair of silk stockings gone and a pair of woollen stockings come) all that is required is the recognition of

identified, alternatively, as an assemblage of antecedent historical events contingently related to a subsequent historical event, or as an assembled passage of antecedent differences which, in virtue of its continuity, constitutes a passage of historical change the outcome of which is a subsequent difference.

It may perhaps be said that this conception of historical change identifies an historically understood past as a past without surprises and devoid of great changes, unable to accommodate abnormal happenings or to reflect 'revolutionary' changes or sudden upheavals; and that an histor-

---

the continuousness of the alteration. We must, of course, put on one side an interpretation of this happening in which it is understood as a succession of actions which achieved their intended outcome. And if we do so, it is clear that, properly speaking, there is no teleology. The woollen stockings are certainly not potential in the silk; nor are they potential in the first woollen stitches. The alteration might at any moment have been suspended without compromising the character of the woollen stitches which are only circumstantially related to their alleged *terminus*. Further, there is nothing to suggest any form of nomological change: the woollen stitches did not cause the woollen stockings. Nor is this an example of *homeostatic* or evolutionary change. And there certainly is a temporal succession of differences related to a circumstantial differential outcome: the woollen stitches touch one another and hold together by reason of their own characters and converge to constitute the outcome. Nevertheless, this cannot be recognized as an example of historical change. Of course, the differences here (the woollen stitches) are unlike antecedent historical events in that they are substantially and not merely formally uniform, differing perhaps only in magnitude. But what is more important is that the identity in terms of which this succession of differences is recognizable as 'change' is the unchanged items in the situation, namely the shape and so on which identifies the stockings as stockings, which survives and is not composed by the differences. Indeed, the change here is, in principle, no different from that in which a pair of white stockings, having fallen into a vat of dye, came out blue, or that in which a pair of stockings shrank in the wash.

ical enquiry, intent upon seeking continuities, unavoidably reduces all change to miniscule movement devoid of 'great' events. And it is, of course, true that a passage of historical change, having no place for normalities or probabilities, has none for the abnormal or the improbable. And 'likelihood' or 'reasonableness' are not general considerations but are always related to circumstances. But the magnitude of a change does not depend upon its relative isolation and is not reduced by its coming to be understood in terms of the details of its mediation; and the rapidity of a change is largely a matter of the scale of the historical enquiry. History written upon a large scale (especially when it is ill-informed of the detail it abridges) is likely to display change more abruptly. And, in general, an historically understood past may be expected to be composed of changes which are neither astonishing nor insignificant, neither out of the blue nor *peu de chose*. But the expression 'great events' belongs rather to the vocabulary of a practical understanding of the past (which may properly distinguish 'watersheds' and 'great leaps forward') than to that of history which has no place for such judgements.

It has been important to distinguish the notion of change employed in an historical enquiry because there is no such thing as change *per se*, and here every distinct notion of change has its counterpart in a different mode of understanding the past. And it is important also to understand that although these categorially different modes of change (and their corresponding pasts) certainly exclude one another, they cannot deny one another: each is secure in terms of its own conditions. Thus, for example, a change may perhaps be recognized as 'miraculous' and, although it may be difficult to ascertain exactly what this means (and it may be a merely rhetorical expression), it certainly attributes to an occurrence something other than the character of an historical event and the outcome of an assembled passage of antecedent historical events. But in seeking to understand a situation as an historical event an historian is not denying the notion of 'miraculous' change, any more than he is denying the notion of 'evolutionary' change: he is merely not employing it. He is doing something else which entails a different notion of change and is consequently concerned with an outcome of a different character: not a miracle but an event.

Moreover, it is in terms of this notion of historical change that the probationary character of historical understanding and the tentative character of an historical event may be recognized not as defects but as characteristics. This product of historical enquiry and imagination is not like the resolution of a jigsaw puzzle, what is on the table being made to correspond to the picture on the lid of the box. There is no such picture and there are no such firm shapes to be picked up and put into their predestined places one at a time. What an historian has are shapes of his own manufacture, more like ambiguous echoes which wind in and out, touch and modify one another; and what he composes is something more like a tune (which may be carried away by the wind) than a neatly fitted together, solid structure. An historical past, no matter whether it is called a *mentalité*, a 'movement', an empire or a war, is a difference composed entirely of contingently related differences which have no conceptual affinity; a continuity of heterogeneous and divergent tensions. And if when an historian has managed to assemble a continuity of change, he identifies it by giving it a name (usually not of his own invention and reluctantly appropriated), calling it 'the Carolingian Empire', 'the Protestant Reformation', 'the Intellectual Revolution of the Seventeenth Century', 'the Peninsular War' or 'European Liberalism', we must understand him to be begging us not to place too much weight upon these identifications, and above all not to confuse his tentative, multiform historical identities with the stark, monolithic products of practical and mythological understanding which these expressions may also identify.

Historical enquiry as a distinguishable mode of enquiry emerged hesitatingly (but not without significant antecedents) in a redirection of an activity inherent in a human

life, that of recalling the past for use in the present and
attending to what it is alleged to say of interest or
instruction in current circumstances. And although there
have been some superb achievements, it has remained a
somewhat uncertain and confused engagement. It did not
and could not supersede or destroy this older and more
compelling practical awareness of the past, and it is not
surprising that even the most severely 'historical' concern
with the past is still liable to be compromised by seeking the
answer to questions which are not historical questions and
by asides and even judgements which belong to some other
mode of understanding. This tentative, usually imperfect,
redirection of attention expressed in the conduct of what, in
virtue of some rough identifying marks, has come to be
recognized as an historical enquiry, must be distinguished
from the engagement of speculative reflection to formulate
the character and conditions of history as a coherent mode
of enquiry and understanding. And we may recognize that
here, as elsewhere (for example in relation to 'scientific'
understanding), the act precedes the reflection, and that
historical enquiry is the invention of historians. Nevertheless, it must be understood that neither is subordinate to
the other. If there had been no such redirection of attention
in respect of the past it would have been difficult (although
not impossible) for a philosopher, with care only for the
necessary conditions for learning about a past which has
not survived and for the conditions of logical coherence, to
have imagined and delineated the formal shape of such a
mode of enquiry and understanding. But although he has
much to learn from historical writings, his engagement is
nothing so simple as that of observing and recording the
practices of historians, and his conclusions do not seek
confirmation in their work. And, on the other hand, in
formulating the conditions of this mode of enquiry he is not
composing directions for the conduct of an historical
enquiry.

The Rule of Law

1

'The rule of law' is a common expression. It is often used, somewhat capriciously, to describe the character of a modern European state or to distinguish some states from others. More often it appears as a description of what a state might perhaps become, or what some people would prefer it to be. But, as with all such shorthand expressions, it is ambiguous and obscure. Let me try to take it to pieces and see what is hidden in it. And I want to begin as near to the bottom as I can and confine myself to what it *must* mean, leaving out of account the desirability or otherwise of the condition it describes and neglecting what it may or may not be made to mean when used as an ideological slogan.

The expression 'the rule of law' relates to human association. It purports to stand for human beings associated in terms of the recognition of certain conditions of association, namely 'laws': human beings joined in an exclusive, specifiable mode of relationship. I shall begin, therefore, with two brief remarks about human relationships in general.

First, relations between persons are apt to be contingent assemblages of a variety of different modes of association. And by a mode of association I mean a categorially distinct kind of relationship, specifiable in terms of its own conditions, which excludes other modes of association but does not deny them. Thus, two persons may be joined, as husband and wife, in a legal mode of relationship, civil or ecclesiastical, but they may also be related in the categorially different terms of love, affection, friendship and so on, and further they may be partners in a business enterprise. And while a teacher and his pupil may have a legal and a commercial relationship, they have also an educational relationship whose terms are neither those of law nor of commerce. In short, while persons may have (and indeed be largely composed of) a variety of different kinds of relationship with others and move between them without confusion, the subject in a *mode* of relationship is always an abstraction, a *persona*, a person in respect of being related to others in terms of distinct and exclusive conditions. And 'the rule of law', standing for a mode of relationship, identifies a *persona* related to others of the same modal character. What is the character of his *persona* and what are the conditions of this mode of association?

Secondly, in spite of their modal diversity, all human relationships have a common character. Human beings are intelligent agents and the terms of all or any of the relationships they enjoy are beliefs and recognitions: not merely what they have learned and understood (or mis-understood), attributed to or assumed about themselves, but what they have seen fit to require of themselves and one another. Human relationships are human inventions, invented *ambulando* in the course of living and imposing conditions upon conduct. Here we have to do with artifice. But a particular mode of human relationship, having been imagined, perhaps elaborated and refined and enjoyed as a practice, may then become the subject of reflection in which its terms and conditions are precisely distiguished. Here, as elsewhere, practice precedes the reflection in which its modal character is formulated. There were friends before Aristotle, Epicurus or Montaigne sought to distinguish the character of friendship. And the 'courtly love' of south-western Europe in the twelfth century was an elaborate, invented, changing practice, celebrated in conduct and vernacular song, long before Andreas Cappilanus wrote his Latin treatise *De Amore* which formulated its modal principles. So this expression, 'the rule of law', stands for a mode of human relationship that has been glimpsed, sketched in a practice, unreflectively and intermittently enjoyed, half-understood, left indistinct: and the task of reflection is not to invent some hitherto unheard of human relationship, but to endow this somewhat vague relationship with a coherent character by distiguishing its conditions as exactly as may be. It stands for a relationship whose sole and exclusive conditions are rules of a certain sort, namely laws. But these laws are not like the 'laws' of chemistry or psychology or those of economics, which purport to predict what will probably happen or to account for what has already happened; they are human inventions that purport to declare the conditions of a human relationship. What is the character of the mode of relationship whose conditions are man-made laws?

2

Perhaps the most rudimentary mode of human relationship is that transactional association in which two or more agents are related solely in seeking and perhaps obtaining the satisfaction of their different current wants: the relation of buyer and seller, of the street flute player and his passing audience, of giver and receiver. What is being sought and perhaps obtained may be distinguished as 'goods' or 'services'. And these wants and satisfactions may be spoken of as 'ends' to be achieved or as 'interests' to be promoted. But, however that may be, this relationship is in terms of wants and their substantive satisfaction by the performance of actions. It is a purposive relationship designed to procure for each of those joined in it an imagined and wished-for substantive (and therefore evanescent) outcome: an intrinsically terminable relationship. And like all human relationship it is abstract – not between persons but between persons in respect of some actual want and its satisfaction: I a would-be buyer of apples and you a would-be seller of apples, I seeking a job and you with a job to offer, he a taxi-driver plying for hire and I wanting to go to Charing Cross.

This transactional mode of association is relationship in

terms of power. The associates are known to each other solely as seekers of substantive satisfactions obtainable only in their responses to one another's conditional offers of satisfactions or threatened refusals to provide, or to assist in providing, a sought-for satisfaction; and they are related in terms of their power to seek or to make such offers or to threaten or resist such refusals, and perhaps also in the recognition and use of such instruments (e.g. money), practices (e.g. promises) or maxims (*caveat emptor*) as they may have devised to promote the effective use of their power. Here, a bid in an auction sale and the patter of a salesman are exercises of power. Thus, this transactional mode of association is, perhaps, recognizable as a kind of causal relationship; actions are performed and utterances made in terms of their expected, hoped-for or predicted substantive consequences.

No doubt it is circumstantially usual in any actual relationship of this sort (although it is by no means always the case)[1] for these transactional encounters to be modified by considerations other than those of power; by the mutual recognition in agents of a *persona* other than a mere seeker of substantive satisfactions, by the intervention of moral scruples or legal obligations; that is, by considerations which if they do not positively hinder the achievement of a sought-for satisfaction, at least have no instrumental relationship to it. But the categorial integrity of what I have called transactional association, understood as an ideal *mode* of association concerned unconditionally with the satisfaction of substantive wants, remains unqualified by any such circumstance.

Another version of this mode of association is that in which agents are joined in seeking to procure the satisfaction of a chosen common want or to promote a common interest. Here, the associates recognize themselves, not as parties related in an engagement of exchange designed to satisfy their different wants, but as colleagues, partners, comrades or accomplices joined in seeking a common

[1] For example, in *la grande peur* in France in the summer of 1789.

substantive satisfaction. They may compose themselves into a fellowship, a guild, a society, a party, a league, an alliance or a community. Their common purpose is to achieve a future, wished-for substantive condition of things that may be simple or complex, a near or a distant prospect, or it may be the continuous promotion of an enduring common interest: the Society for the Propagation of Christian Knowledge, the Anti-Bloodsports League, the Licensed Victuallers Association. And even an inward-looking association that has no substantive purpose (a society of 'friends') may acquire this character if its existence is opposed or threatened.

Association here is the assemblage of an aggregate of power to compose a corporate or an associational identity designed to procure a wished-for satisfaction. It is constituted in the choice and recognition of a common purpose to the pursuit of which each associate undertakes to devote a quantum of his power; that is, his time, energy, means, skill and so on. The associates are *personae*, persons in respect of their devotion to the common cause. The engagement occupies time, it is a call upon resources, it looks to a future, it is inherently terminable and may terminate with the achievement of its purpose or the dissolution of the association. In short, the *mode* of association here is what I have called transactional. The associates are joined in transactions among themselves in which their various skills are directed to the service of the common cause. And the cause itself is pursued in transaction with others who belong to other such associations or to none.

Since the associational concern in this version of transactional relationship is to assemble power as an efficient means for achieving an end, and since its resources are the various contributions of its members, it may be expected to have some kind of organization besides the bare common recognition of the end to be pursued. There may be articles of association designed to exclude those who might hinder the undertaking, a constitution, statutory meetings to determine policy, offices of responsibility and so on. But these arrangements, practices, rules and routines are no more than the prudential disposition of the available resources, instrumental to the pursuit of the common purpose and desirable in terms of their utility, which itself lies in their uninterrupted functionality. And because they have no independent status as conditions of association and introduce no new considerations, they are incapable of qualifying the *mode* of association which remains relationship in terms of the wish and the power to procure a substantive satisfaction. And while any such band of associates may give recognition to non-instrumental moral or legal considerations, this again does not qualify the integrity of their transactional relationship as a distinct mode of association.

Here, then, is a *persona* – not a notional 'natural' man condemned to seek his own felicity, a balance of pleasure over pain or 'survival', but one composed exclusively of circumstantial wants and interests, concerned to satisfy and to promote them in transactions with others and identified in terms of a capacity to do so. Such endeavour has an inevitable self-reference, but it is not at all necessary that this character should be what is vulgarly called a 'self-seeking' *persona*. The substantive satisfaction sought may be the prosperity of another or the welfare of the New Forest ponies; but this does not qualify the mode of association. And here is a distinct mode of association: relationship in terms of wants and substantive satisfactions which occupies time and looks to a future, in which the means employed may include instrumental rules, arrangements and practices, but which is subject to no other considerations save those of power to achieve a purpose.

But this, clearly, is not the *persona* and not the mode of association we are looking for. What we are seeking is an alleged mode of association in which the associates are expressly and exclusively related in terms of the recognition of rules of conduct of a certain kind, namely 'laws'. And what we have here is associates related expressly and exclusively in terms of seeking to satisfy substantive wants and their power to do so. In this *mode* of association there is nothing whatever to correspond to the expression 'the rule of law': there is only Purpose, Plan, Policy and Power.[2] Let us try again.

3

Consider the relationship entailed in playing a game: chess, tennis or cricket.

There is, first, the *persona* of a competitor. He is engaged in a purposive enterprise: the pursuit of a wished-for substantive satisfaction. He is out to win. He may perhaps want to exercise his mind (chess as an alternative to doing a puzzle), or his muscles (playing tennis as an alternative to jogging), but unless he behaves as a competitor there is no game. How impossible it is to play tennis with an opponent who does not even try to win. The engagement takes time, it is pursued in the performance of a succession of actions and it has a terminus. This *persona* is related to his competitors and to his fellows (if any) in terms of power; that is, in the exercise of his relative skill in performing actions to procure the satisfaction he seeks. These are the terms in which a 'good' player is distinguished from one not so good. And if he is a member of a team, these are the terms in which he is understood and valued by his fellows. This skill is various, but its more general features may, in part, be formulated in terms of instrumental precepts or maxims such as those enunciated by a trainer or a coach. These precepts are often thought of as rules, but if so they

[2] The contention that even this mode of association cannot escape the rule of law – that the choice and performance of actions in pursuit of substantive satisfactions is subject to the 'laws of history' or of physics, and that success here is subject to the 'law of averages' or the 'law of the strongest' – is, of course, irrelevant. This is not the kind of law referred to in the expression 'the rule of law'.

should be recognized as instrumental injunctions which point to actions or ploys advantageous in pursuing a wished-for purpose and regarded as more or less valuable in respect of an extended experience of their uninterrupted functionality. Thus, to be told to keep a straight bat is not to be directed to one of the 'rules of cricket' but to be made aware of a valuable prudential consideration related to a successful batsman.

Superimposed upon this active, purposeful *persona* is another, constituted not in terms of the performance of actions or the enjoyment of a skill in pursuing a substantive satisfaction, but in terms of the recognition of the game. And what is this game? It is nothing other than a set of rules. And what are these rules? They are certainly not precepts that distinguish between imagined actions in terms of their propensity to procure a wished-for future satisfaction. They are not guides to the effective use of power, they do not award advantages or disadvantages to the competitors and they are not the terms in which the better and worse players are distinguished. Nor do they point to a purpose additional or alternative to that of a competitor. They are not commands to do or to forbear. Subscription to these rules is not itself a possible substantive action; it is the observance of adverbial qualifications imposed upon the only actions there are, namely, those in which a competitor uses his skill to seek a satisfaction. These rules have been made in a procedure of deliberation and may be changed or modified. They exist and are known in advance of any occasion of play and they subsist independently of any such occasion. To be related in terms of these non-instrumental rules is to be related in a mutual obligation to observe the conditions which themselves constitute the game, an obligation which cannot be evaded on the grounds of disapproval of or conscientious objection to what they prescribe and which may be symbolically expressed in deference to their custodian: an umpire or a referee. There may be penalties annexed to the non-observance of these rules, but the rules themselves do not presume recalcitrance and the obligation to subscribe to them is not merely an obligation to submit to a penalty.

And further, the rules of a game exhibit the dual character of all genuine rules. They may be considered in respect of their authenticity or in respect of the desirability of the conditions they prescribe. And here each of these considerations appears in a characteristic shape. For those engaged in play, the first consideration – the authenticity of a rule – is all that matters. And here, where the rules are few, simple and familiar, this may be decided without elaborate enquiry by reference to a rule-book; or, if the book allows alternatives, it may be settled on the occasion by agreement between the players before the play begins. Since the rules of a game are the arbitrary conditions of an autonomous engagement, they cannot all at once be declared undesirable, and the consideration of the desirability of the condition prescribed by any of them is a similarly limited concern. It may be thought that a rule is unduly burdensome, that it tends to 'spoil the game' and should on that account be changed; but there are no considerations in terms of which it might be said, in any extended sense, to be 'unfair'. The expression 'fair play' does not invoke considerations of 'justice'; it means neither more nor less than to play *this* game conscientiously according to its authentic rules. And of course such rules cannot include a rule that the game should or should not be played.

The players of a game are, then, related in two categorially distinct modes of association. One is an actual, terminable relationship of assignable contestants identified in terms of their several powers to pursue, in a succession of self-chosen actions, a substantive outcome. It is a relationship located in respect of a place and a time and it is exhausted on the occasion. The other is an ideal relationship, invoked on the occasion of a substantive contest, but subsisting in advance and independently of any such occasion and not exhausted on the occasion. And it is this second relationship that affords us a glimpse of a mode of association expressly and exclusively in terms of the recognition of rules. But it is no more than a glimpse. There is some way to go before the full character of association in terms of the rule of law comes into view. Nevertheless, we may claim already to have learned something of the meaning of the expression. Let me collect it.

4

Maxims, advices, instructions, pleas, warnings or admonitions are either utterances spoken at large in reference to some general circumstance understood in terms of its kind and purporting to recommend the substantive response it should or should not receive if ever it arose, or they are addressed to an assignable agent advising him how to respond to the situation in which he finds himself. Thus, one of the *Comments of Bagshot* reads: 'Advice to the poor: in all the emergencies of life act as if you were rich.' Or the solicitor's account I found in my father's papers: 'January 30th 1892. To Advice to let sleeping dogs lie: One guinea.' Or the Duke of Wellington's reply to a correspondent: 'From what you say you seem to have got yourself into a damned difficult situation and you must do your best to get out of it.'

Such utterances and their like differ from rules in two important respects. First, their idiom is prudential. They may urge those to whom they are addressed to do this rather than that, to do something rather than nothing or to do nothing rather than something, but always on consequential grounds. Their concern is with actions as the means for achieving wished-for substantive satisfaction or for avoiding unwanted outcomes, whereas a rule is related to no substantive end, being concerned with the propriety of conduct, not its expediency. Secondly, the validity of a recommendation contained in a maxim or precept and its desirability or worth as a piece of advice are indistinguishable; both lie in its sagacity or utility – that is, in the outcome of following it being (or being likely to be) the substantive satisfaction sought. Whereas the validity of a rule lies in its authenticity, which may be established or rebutted only in terms of considerations of a categorially different kind from those which may be invoked in defending or rebutting its desirability, and these considerations do not relate to its aptitude for achieving a substantive end.

At the other extreme, a rule is not itself a command. First, a command or an order is an utterance addressed to an assignable agent; whereas a rule, if it is thought of as an utterance, is addressed to an unknown (and in part a yet unborn) audience. It has a jurisdiction and it relates indifferently and continuously to all who fall, or may in future fall, within this jurisdiction. Secondly, a command is itself an action in response to a particular situation and is used up on the occasion; whereas a rule subsists and is known in advance of the hypothetical situations to which it may subsequently be found to relate and is not used up in being invoked or subscribed to. Thirdly, a command is an injunction to perform a substantive action and it calls for obedience; that is, the performance of the action it specifies. Whereas rules assume agents wishing to perform and performing self-chosen actions in pursuit of substantive satisfactions and they stipulate, not the performance of some alternative action, but subscription to adverbial conditions in the performance of all or any actions. The response to a rule cannot be obedience; it is adequate subscription to the conditions it prescribes. Fourthly, a command, properly speaking,[3] is an authoritative utterance designed to procure a substantive condition of things (the action performed and perhaps the wished-for and expected more distant outcome), and its validity lies neither in the character or quality of what is commanded, nor in any power to penalize disobedience which may be annexed to it, but solely in its authority or authenticity. And this authenticity may be determined only by reference

[3] That is, distinguished from a 'demand' such as 'Your money or your life', which is an expression merely of power.

to a rule. Commands are not themselves rules, but they postulate association in terms of rules. Competence to command belongs to an office, a *persona* identified in terms of rules; and only a *persona* identified in terms of obligations to obey may be the subject of a command.

Further, a rule is not merely a standard or criterion in terms of which to weigh, measure and identify the propriety of actions. It does not merely distinguish between right and wrong in conduct; it is an authoritative prescription of conditions to be subscribed to in acting and its counterpart is an *obligation* to subscribe to these conditions. But to have such an obligation is not merely to feel constrained, nor is it to be confused with having a disposition usually to comply with what a rule prescribes – what has been called 'a habit of obedience'. It is neither more nor less than an acknowledgement of the authenticity of the rule. And just as the authenticity or authority of a rule relates neither to approval of what it prescribes nor to any remuneratory or punitive consequences that may be expected to follow compliance or non-compliance with its prescriptions, so the obligation it entails is related neither to approval of what it prescribes nor to a hope or a fear in respect of the consequences of observance or non-observance. And this obligation is not denied in a failure to comply or even in a refusal to comply. What, in the first place, association in terms of rules calls for is a ready means of ascertaining their authenticity.

Nevertheless, rules may also be appreciated in respect of what they prescribe. This is what must occupy the attention of the makers of rules and it may be the legitimate concern of others. Since what a rule prescribes is an obligation to subscribe to non-instrumental adverbial conditions in the performance of the self-chosen actions of all who fall within its jurisdiction, what falls to be appreciated here is the actual conditions it obligates them to observe. Among makers of rules this may invoke a variety of prudential and consequential considerations (such as the difficulty or probable cost of detecting a delinquency), but for them and for others its central concern is with what may be called, somewhat loosely, the 'evaluation' of these conditions distinguished from the determination of their authenticity. By this I mean not merely the consistency of a rule with the others that compose the set of rules to which it belongs or is designed to belong, but its virtue as a contribution to the shape of this set of rules as the desirable conditions of an invented pattern of non-instrumental human relationships. Where (as in a game) this shape is arbitrary this evaluative engagement is strictly limited: there is no place for general principles, much less universal criteria of desirability. But clearly this limitation is not inherent in the notion of a rule and evaluation may be an extensive enterprise.

Finally, two further considerations are at least intimated in what we may learn from games about association in terms of rules. First, disputes may arise as to whether or not, on a certain occasion, the conditions of a rule have been adequately observed, and some authoritative procedure is required to settle them. And secondly, since such association depends, in part, upon the rules being generally observed, penalties annexed to their non-observance may be required. But, of course, while a wish to avoid a penalty may be a reason for conformity, it cannot be the ground of the obligation to conform.

So far, then, asssociation in terms of rules appears as relationship in respect of authoritative prescriptions which have a certain jurisdiction and an ascertainable authenticity. They assume agents engaged in self-chosen actions to promote or procure various substantive satisfactions and they impose obligations upon them to observe certain adverbial conditions in performing all or any of these actions. These rules are not designed to promote or to impede the achievement of these satisfactions and are incapable of doing so, and they are not instrumental to the achievement of a substantive purpose of their own. And these obligations may or may not be observed, but they are not denied in a failure to observe them.

This is the situation of the players of a game. But, as I have suggested, a game provides a somewhat limited example of this mode of association. The engagement is intermittent and undertaken at will. The situation of competing for the enjoyment of a single and final satisfaction within a given period of time is peculiar. The actions to which the rules relate are few and simple and the rules of a game (themselves few and simple) are arbitrary; the desirability of what a particular rule prescribes is determined in its relation to the others. Their authenticity is usually unquestioned but an enquiry into it beyond reference to a rule-book would be difficult to pursue. The variety of the ways in which a rule of a game may be adequately observed is strictly limited, and the penalties imposed for a breach of the rules have the somewhat odd appearance of being reparations for disadvantages suffered. And the rules themselves have an unusual status: although the sought-for satisfaction (winning) cannot, of course, be achieved merely by observing the rules, it is nevertheless defined in terms of rules.

Let us consider what at least is a less intermittent example of this mode of association: what may be called moral association.

5

Moral association is relationship of human beings in terms of the mutual recognition of certain conditions which not only specify moral right and wrong in conduct, but are prescriptions of obligations. It assumes agents to be related transactionally in performing actions to satisfy their several wants and imposes on all such engagements the obligation to observe certain conditions. These conditions are neither instrumental to the achievement of substantive satisfactions, nor do they have a substantive purpose of their own. Thus, moral association is not only an abstract relationship, a relationship of *personae*, but the terms of the abstraction are modally different from those of association for the purpose of satisfying wants.

As it comes to us and as we learn it, a morality is not a list of licences and prohibitions but an everyday practice; that is, a vernacular language of intercourse. Like any other language in its use, it is never fixed and finished. But although it may be criticized and modified in detail it can never be rejected *in toto* and replaced by another. It may be spoken with various degrees of *sprachgefühl*, but it can never tell us what to say or to do, only how we should say or do what we wish to say or do. Thus moral conduct, conduct in respect of its recognition of the considerations of a morality, is a kind of literacy. And just as considerations of literacy do not themselves compose utterances, and just as a practice can never itself be performed, so we may act morally but no actual performance can be specified in exclusively moral terms.

Besides participating in moral association there are various engagements we may undertake in respect of a morality: three in particular.

First, we may ignore the actual obligatory conditions prescribed in a morality and reflect upon the character of moral relationship as a mode of association; that is, formulate various propositions about moral authority and obligation. This is the engagement of a moral philosopher as distinct from that of a moralist. One of its main concerns is to specify the *persona* entailed in this mode of relationship. And it may, perhaps, throw up such propositions as that this *persona* is not that of an agent transactionally seeking the satisfaction of his wants, or that the exclusive concern of moral considerations is with the motives in which actions are performed.

Secondly, a moral practice may be displayed as the conditional responses of an ideal *persona*: for example, Newman's characterization of a 'gentleman' as a *persona* composed, not of propensities to want or to do this rather than that, but of the recognition of certain considerations in whatever he may choose to do.

Thirdly, a moral practice may be abridged and epito-mized and displayed as a set of rules. This, no doubt, is a somewhat crude undertaking, but if we pursue it what may come into view is a not unrecognizable example of associa-tion in terms of the acknowledgement of rules.

The rules to which a moral practice may perhaps be reduced are not prudential directions, instructions or warnings about what to do and what not to do in relation to likely consequences: they enunciate obligations. They are not merely standards or criteria of right and wrong in conduct: they impose obligations. They are not commands addressed to assignable agents to perform specified actions designed to have substantive outcomes: they subsist in advance of and in ignorance of the circumstances to which they may relate and they are not used up in being invoked. What they prescribe is the obligation to observe adverbial conditions in performing self-chosen actions – conditions that, of course, cannot themselves be performed. These conditions are not instrumental to the achievement of the satisfactions sought for in the performances to which they relate, and they have no substantive purpose or end of their own to procure or promote. And failure, or even refusal, to subscribe to these conditions is not a denial of the obliga-tion to do so. In short, these have the appearance of being genuine rules in which a moral practice has been reduced to specifiable duties.

Nevertheless, there are considerations that make it difficult to recognize moral relationship as exclusively in terms of rules. We may put on one side the simple confusion in which moral rules are mistaken for directions instrumental to the achievement of a variously specified substantive condition of things: 'the good', for example, identified with the prosperity of the associates or the maximization of the pleasurable sensations of the associ-ates and their pet animals. But the rigidity of a morality reduced to rules, its appearance of turning moral consid-erations into mere protocol invites the revulsion in which it is translated into a meaningless assemblage of absolute 'rights', or the nonconformity which seeks release in a claim to be obligated by 'conscience', or in the declarations of a self-conscious 'immoralist' who thinks that these precise rules of grammar somehow stand in the way of his having a 'style' of his own. Moreover, where there is nothing but rules their unavoidable indeterminancy calls for a procedure of casuistry in which they are related to circumstantial occasions; and (apart from the alleged destruction of 'the moral consciousness' entailed in a moral casuistry) is there not something lacking where there is no authoritative provision for it and every man must do his own casuistry for himself or accept the conclusions of some self-appointed moralist? And again, is there not something lacking to alleged association in terms of rules where there are no penalties annexed to the inadequate observance of their conditions save the condemnation of the aggrieved, the disapproval of the bystander or the arbitrary outlawry of social ostracism?

But the chief consideration that stands in the way of recognizing moral association as relationship in terms of rules is the difficulty of determining the authenticity of an alleged moral rule and of distinguishing this from the recognition of the 'rightness' of the conditions it prescribes. These difficulties never invade the rule of a game: any question of their authenticity is settled by an accepted rulebook, and the arbitrary character of the conditions prescribed by the rules of a game precludes anything but a strictly relativist consideration of their 'rightness', and there is no temptation to confuse the two. But in respect of a morality reduced to rules, where both authenticity and 'rightness' are prime and contentious considerations there is no easy solution. Indeed, it would be difficult to find a moralist who, if he understood moral relationship as association in terms of rules, was not disposed to abandon authenticity in favour of 'rightness' as the ground of moral obligation. Thus William of Ockham could recognize the authority of a moral rule in terms of its authenticity as the voluntary utterance of a God, the divinity of whose will was itself also a guarantee of the 'rightness' of whatever it prescribed. And others have ostensibly clung to the notion of the authenticity of a moral rule but placed it elsewhere in its correspondence with a rational natural law, in the necessary conditions of 'self-realization' or in 'conscience', each of which is also a disguised guarantee of its 'rightness'; or they have gone the whole hog and have declared the notion of authenticity redundant. In short, one way or another moral relationship as association in terms of rules has remained a cloudy or contentious notion in which it is difficult to distinguish authenticity from 'rightness'. But if we must look elsewhere for the mode of association which the expression 'the rule of law' identifies we may carry with us the perception that it must be a mode of association in which *lex* (a rule understood in terms of its authenticity) and *jus* (a rule understood in terms of the 'rightness' or 'justice' of what it prescribes) are both recognized but are not confused.

6

The expression 'the rule of law', taken precisely, stands for a mode of moral association exclusively in terms of the recognition of the authority of known, non-instrumental rules (that is, laws) which impose obligations to subscribe to adverbial conditions in the performance of the self-chosen actions of all who fall within their jurisdiction. This mode of association may be opprobriously branded as 'legalistic' and other modes may be considered more interesting or more profitable, but this I think is what the rule of law must mean. Like all other modes of association it is an abstract relationship of *personae* – persons solely in respect of being alike and without exception the subjects of these obligations to one another.

Such persons may be in all other respects total strangers to one another. Or, in the exercise of some other *persona*, they may be temporarily or durably joined with some

On History

"The Tower of Babel"
- deprived, envy, wants

others in some other mode of relationship, chosen and terminable at will or by agreement: in transactions to procure substantive satisfactions, in the exchange of services, in giving and receiving, in sharing and expressing religious beliefs, or in promoting a common *interest*. Indeed, there is no end to the number and variety of the minorities of interest into which they may circumstantially compose themselves or the collocations (sex, family, race, profession, hobby and so on) in terms of which they may from time to time recognize themselves. But in all these respects and in all these activities, where there is also relationship in terms of the rule of law, they remain, in that respect, indistinguishably and inescapably related in terms of the conditions prescribed by laws which are not designed to promote or to hinder the pursuit of any substantive interest and which consequently do not and cannot afford any of them recognition. Nor may relationship in respect of the rule of law be itself association to promote or procure a common substantive satisfaction. For the terms of such purposive association would not be obligations to subscribe to adverbial conditions while performing diverse and self-chosen actions, but undertakings to perform such actions as might be judged instrumental to the pursuit and achievement of a chosen common end; and this is impossible. Finally, relationship in terms of the rule of law cannot be association in respect of the common recognition of the desirability of the conditions prescribed in all or any of the laws, or of some quality of 'rightness' or 'justice' or 'reasonableness' they may be deemed to possess, or of the associates always or usually subscribing to these conditions, or of some notional power to compel such subscription, or of whatever penalties are annexed to non-subscription. The sole terms of this relationship are the recognition of the authority or authenticity of the laws.

Thus, the first condition of this mode of association is for the associates to know what the laws are and to have a procedure, as little speculative as may be, for ascertaining their authenticity and that of the obligations they prescribe. And this is satisfied only where laws have been deliberately enacted or appropriated and may be deliberately altered or repealed by persons in respect of their occupation of an exclusively legislative office and following a recognized procedure; where the sole recognition of the authenticity of a law is that expressed in an acknowledgement that it has been properly enacted; where this acknowledgement does not entail approval of what the law prescribes; and where there is no other independent office authorized to declare a law inauthentic on account of what it prescribes. In short, the first condition of the rule of law is a 'sovereign' legislative office.

Nevertheless, the rule of law does not itself specify any particular constitution or procedure in respect of this legislative office. It does not itself stipulate who shall occupy it, the rules in terms of which it may properly be occupied, or the procedure to be followed in enacting law. It requires only that these should themselves be matters of law. And it attributes a *persona* to the occupant or occupants of this office which reflects the engagement of enacting authentic rules: a *persona* without interests of its own and not representative of the interests of others. That is, a *persona* which is the counterpart of the *persona* of those related in terms of the rule of law.

But while a legislative office recognized as the maker and custodian of the law and as the condition of its authenticity is necessary for association in terms of the rule of law, it is not necessary that this law should be codified, nor is it necessary for this office to be the sole *source* of law. Nevertheless, where a rule is recognized to be *mos majorum* (or distinguished as a 'common law', perhaps of unknown origin), it must be lodged within the custody of the legislative office. Its authority cannot lie in its antiquity, in its current availability, its traditional acceptance or in the recognition of the desirability of what it prescribes; its authenticity derives from a presumption, namely, that it cannot resist appropriation, rejection or emendation in a legislative enactment.

The rule of law, then, as a mode of human relationship, postulates an office with authority to make law. There are, of course, a variety of ways in which such an office might be erected. But, so far as the mode of association is concerned, all that need be observed is that, since this authority cannot be identified with any natural quality (virtue, prudence, wisdom, charisma and so on) possessed by or attributed to its contingent occupants, or inferred from any such quality, it must be an endowment of the office itself; that since it is an authority to create obligations, it must be conferred in the acknowledgement of those obligated; and that since it is an antecedent authorization to make law, it cannot be identified with approval of what the law prescribes.[4] Beyond this, the expression 'the rule of law' denotes a self-sustained, notionally self-consistent, mode of human association in terms of the recognition of the authority or authenticity of enacted laws and the obligations they prescribe in which the considerations in terms of which the authenticity of a law may be confirmed or rebutted are themselves enacted law;[5] in which the jurisdiction of the law is itself a matter of law; and in which the necessary condition that the associates be aware of the obligations the law imposes is subsumed under the principle that ignorance of the law is no defence against the imputation of having failed to observe its prescriptions.

A law, in order to be recognized as a law properly

[4] A usurper and a tyrant are alike without authority, but for different reasons. A usurper may have the disinterested *persona* required of a legislator but he cannot make authentic law because he does not properly occupy the legislative office. A tyrant may properly occupy the office but he uses his occupation to promote *interests*, chiefly his own, and therefore does not make genuine law.

[5] That 'law regulates its own creation' is not a paradox but a truism.

speaking, must have ascertainable authority. But the conditions it imposes upon conduct certainly have qualities other than, and distinct from, the obligatory character they derive from the authenticity of their enactment. And any account of this mode of association must recognize these qualities. The most important of them is that denoted by the words 'justice' and 'injustice' – *jus* and *injus*. Indeed, a notion of *jus* may be said to be presupposed in the rule of law. And since *jus* (among much else) is a consideration invoked in the deliberation that goes to the making of law, this is perhaps the appropriate place to say something about it. What exactly is the notion of *jus* postulated in the rule of law?

In the rule of law, the constitution of the legislative office is neither more nor less than that which endows law with authenticity, consequently the *jus* or *injus* of what is enacted cannot be inferred from such a constitution or procedure. Thus, to favour a so-called 'democratically elected' legislature is to express a belief that its authority to enact laws will be more confidently acknowledgeable than that of a legislature assembled and constituted in any other manner; it forecasts nothing whatever about the *jus* or *injus* of its enactments. For that we must look elsewhere.

There are some considerations that are often and understandably identified as considerations of *jus* but are in fact inherent in the notion, not of a just law, but of law itself. They are conditions which distinguish a legal order and in default of which whatever purports to be a legal order is not what it purports to be: rules not secret or retrospective, no obligations save those imposed by law, all associates equally and without exception subject to the obligations imposed by law, no outlawry, and so on. It is only in respect of these considerations and their like that it may perhaps be said that *lex injusta non est lex*. And there are also similar considerations concerned with adjudicating cases (for example, *audire alteram partem*), which we shall come to later.

Beyond this, the *jus* or *injus* of a law is composed of

considerations in terms of which a law may be recognized, not merely as properly enacted, but as proper or not improper to be or to have been enacted; beliefs and opinions invoked in considering the propriety of the conditions prescribed in a particular law. *Jus* or *injus*, here, is an attribute neither of the mode of association, nor of the totality of the rules which may constitute the current conditions of such an association, nor of the performance of a legislator, but only of what a particular law prescribes. Nor is it related to a forecast of its likely substantive consequences: whether or not it will tumble the heavens. To these it is indifferent. Further, law is not concerned with the merits of different interests, with satisfying substantive wants, with the promotion of prosperity, the elimination of waste, the equal or differential distribution of reputed benefits or opportunities, with arbitrating competing claims to advantages or satisfactions, or with the promotion of a condition of things recognized as the common good. Consequently, the *jus* of a law cannot be identified with the successful provision of these or any other substantive benefits, measured by the efficiency or expedition with which they are provided or the 'fairness' with which they are distributed. Nor can law be concerned with the provision or the assurance of the enjoyment of benefits alleged to be desired by all. If there are such universally acknowledged 'natural' goods (and biological survival has been said to be among them), law cannot be concerned with promoting them unconditionally. Its business with these, or any other sought-for satisfactions, is to prescribe obligatory conditions to be observed in seeking them. In short, the propriety which identifies the *jus* of *lex* must be composed of moral, non-instrumental considerations. Nevertheless, the conditions a law imposes upon conduct cannot concern the supreme moral consideration which relates to the sentiments or motives in which actions are performed. The *jus* of *lex* cannot specify anything so grand as the conditions of 'human excellence' or of human 'self-realization'. But if *dike* is something more commonplace than *aidos*, it is certainly a moral and not a prudential consideration.

Nevertheless, theorists of the rule of law have experienced some difficulty in deciding upon the considerations in terms of which the prescriptions of man-made law may be recognized to be 'just' or not 'unjust'. The main thrust of the enterprise has been to seek them in the reflection that *lex* throws back of the provisions of an inherently just 'higher' or 'fundamental' law, a Law of Nature or of God, either discerned in rational moral deliberation or (in the Ockhamist version) recognized as the prescriptions of the arbitrary 'will' of a divine legislator. And for the convenience of having a more readily available norm of justice, the *jus* of *lex* has often been identified with its reflection of (or absence of conflict with) the requirements of a 'basic law', not fetched from Sinai but the product of human deliberation, which itself encapsulates the provisions of the more speculative 'higher' law. Here there may be a variety of beliefs in respect of the authority of this 'higher' law, but there is no confusion: it is *law*. And the *jus* of *lex* is sought in its relation to the provisions of a genuine law which (therefore) is concerned, not with the approval or disapproval of actions, but with the prescription of conditions to be observed in performing self-chosen actions, and which differ from the provisions of *lex* only in respect of their greater generality.

On the other hand, the *jus* of the prescriptions of *lex* has been said to lie in their conformity with a set of 'fundamental values', 'the basic requirements of practical reasonableness in human conduct', in a set of inviolable 'human rights' or of 'unconditional human liberties'. Here there is some confusion. It is not at all clear how the necessarily conditional prescriptions of *lex* can derive their *jus* from their conformity (or absence of conflict) with a set of unconditional 'values', 'rights' or 'liberties', etc. Indeed, it is logically impossible that this should be the case. Moreover, those who seek the *jus* of *lex* in these alleged

unconditionals of reasonable or worthwhile human existence often identify them as interests or substantive satisfactions (claims to go on living, to procreate, to have one's
elementary needs provided for and so on) which *lex*, in
order to be recognized as 'just', must promote or at least not
hinder. And this, of course, denies to *lex* its character of a
non-instrumental rule. But at the centre of both these
versions of this enterprise is the endeavour to discern
demonstrable, unambiguous and universal criteria in terms
of which to determine the *jus* of *lex*.

But whether or not such certainty and universality are
attainable in this or any other manner, it may be said that
association in terms of the rule of law has no need of them.
First, it postulates a distinction between *jus* and the
procedural considerations in respect of which to determine
the authenticity of a law. Secondly, it recognizes the formal
principles of a legal order which may be said to be
themselves principles of 'justice'. And beyond this it may
float upon the acknowledgement that the considerations in
terms of which the *jus* of *lex* may be discerned are neither
arbitrary, nor unchanging, nor uncontentious, and that
they are the product of a moral experience which is never
without tensions and internal discrepancies. What this
mode of association requires for determining the *jus* of a
law is not a set of abstract criteria but an appropriately
argumentative form of discourse in which to deliberate the
matter; that is, a form of moral discourse, not concerned
generally with right and wrong in human conduct, but
focused narrowly upon the kind of conditional obligations
a law may impose, undistracted by prudential and consequential considerations, and insulated from the spurious
claims of conscientious objection, of minorities for excep-
tional treatment and, so far as may be, from current moral
idiocies. And what it has no room for is either a so-called
Bill of Rights (that is, alleged unconditional principles of *jus*
masquerading as themselves law), or an independent office
and apparatus charged with considering the *jus* of a law

and authorized to declare a law to be inauthentic if it were found to be 'unjust'. Such considerations and institutions may perhaps have an appropriate place where association is in terms of *interests* and '*jus*' is no more than an equitable accommodation of interests to one another, but they have no place whatever in association in terms of the rule of law.

But to return to our consideration of the offices necessary for this mode of association.

Laws are unavoidably indeterminate prescriptions of general adverbial obligations. They subsist in advance and in necessary ignorance of the future contingent situations to which they may be found to relate. And even if these prescriptions were 'certain' (that is, as free as may be from ambiguity and conflict with one another) they could not themselves declare their meaning in respect of any circumstantial situation. Therefore, the second necessary condition of association in terms of the rule of law is an office endowed with authority and charged with the duty to ascertain (according to some conditional rules of evidence) what had been said or done on a particular occasion brought to its notice because it is alleged not to have subscribed adequately to an obligation imposed by law; to determine whether or not what was said or done on that occasion had or had not observed the legal obligation it was required to observe; and perhaps to assign a penalty or declare a remedy for this inadequate subscription. In short, what is required is a judicial office, a court of law concerned with considering actual performances solely in respect of their legality.

The engagement of such a court is deliberative, but the considerations and procedure here are categorially different from those of the deliberation entailed in making a law.[6] Whereas a legislator deliberates the desirability of a

[6] Montesquieu, not always a sure-footed theorist of the rule of law, identified this distinction, in the epistemological convention of his time, as a distinction between the kind of 'will' exercised respectively by a legislator and a judge: the one a *volonté générale*

change in some part of the existing system of general obligations and how this change may be accommodated within the system of general obligations, a court of law is concerned with a particular contingent action or utterance in respect of its conformity with the conditions of existing obligations. It may consider only an actual, not an imaginary or a conjectured, occurrence; it will consider only an occurrence in respect of which there is alleged to have been a breach of the law; it must reach a conclusion, and whatever this is the law remains unimpaired. Its task is to relate a general statement of conditional obligation to an occurrence in terms of what *distinguishes* it from other occurrences. Deliberation, here, is an exercise in retrospective casuistry.

Like all casuistical enterprise, this is •a devious engagement.[7] But it is governed by a procedure composed of rules, conventions, uses, presumptions and so on,

---

and the other a *volonté particulière*. And although he calls what follows where either office operates in the manner of the other (and particularly where a Dworkinesque judge usurps the office of legislator), a destruction of *liberté*, he recognizes this failure to observe a so-called 'separation of powers' (which properly speaking is a distinction of authorities) to be a category confusion which subverts the character of relationship in terms of the rule of law.

[7] Aristotle thought it to be necessary only when a situation revealed itself to be an 'exception' to a law which (like all laws) was liable to be defective because it could be designed to relate only to 'the majority of cases'. And such exceptions were to be dealt with by considering 'what the lawgiver would do if he were present' and 'what he would have provided in the law if the case had occurred to him' (*Eth. Nic.* V, 10, 4–6).

Montaigne, on the other hand, thought it to be impossible: *Il y a peu de relations de nos actions, qui sont en perpetuelle mutation, avec les loix fixes et immobiles.* But, then, he thought that laws prescribed substantive actions, not conditions to be observed in acting. And he was confronted with the dilemma either of having as many laws as there were possible actions (a shoe for every

designed to focus attention upon the relevant considerations. Since this court is concerned with disputes about conditional responsibilities and where they lay on a particular occasion, it is not concerned to arbitrate between competing substantive interests: suitors to this court are *persona* related in terms of the rule of law and, like the court itself, have no 'interests'. In seeking the meaning of a law in relation to a contingent occurrence this court cannot entertain speculations about the intentions of legislators or conjectures about how they would decide the case: to make law and to adjudicate a case are categorially different engagements. Nor may it regard itself as the custodian of a public policy or interest in favour of which (when all else fails) to resolve the disputed obligation: association in terms of the rule of law, although it may have a public prosecutor as a suitor to a court, knows nothing of a 'public interest' save the sum of the obligations imposed by law. Nor may it consider a case in terms of so-called substantive 'rights' claimed as a matter of *jus* in some current moral opinion: the right to speak, to be informed, to enjoy an equal opportunity or the advantage of a handicap. The rule of law knows nothing of unconditional 'rights'. Nor again, may the decisions of a court be attributed to what is called the 'subjective opinion' of the adjudicator about what is 'just'. Leaving on one side the mistaken notion that 'subjectivity' is not both a universal and usually an insignificant characteristic of every opinion about anything whatever, in a court of law 'justice' must exhibit itself as the conclusion of an argument designed to show as best it may that *this* is the meaning of the law in respect of this occurrence. And although it may belong to the procedure of such a court to take account of decisions in earlier allegedly similar cases, it will not recognize them as

---

foot), or of suffering the inevitable inconsequent sophistries of lawyers who are like children playing with quicksilver: the more they try to press it into a coherent shape the more it scatters (*De l'Expérience, Essais III*, xiii).

precedents to be followed: its concern will be with the analogical force of the distinctions they invoked. In respect of the rule of law the expression 'case law' is a solecism. Briefly then, this procedure and these considerations identify the business of the court to be neither more nor less than that of declaring the meaning of a law in respect of a contingent occurrence.[8] Of course, the rules of this procedure cannot themselves announce such conclusion, any more than a law can itself declare its meaning in respect of a contingent occurrence, but they distinguish the casuistical engagement of a court of law from the exercise of what has been called 'a sovereign prerogative of arbitrary choice'.

Association in terms of the rule of law does not presume recalcitrance on the part of its members. Nevertheless, it provides, not so much for the enforcement of the law (which is a nearly meaningless expression), as for the punishment of those convicted of failure to observe their obligations and perhaps something by way of remedy for the substantive damage attributable to delinquency. A failure to subscribe adequately to an obligation imposed by law, unlike the breach of a taboo, does not carry with it an automatic penalty, the suffering of which may exculpate the delinquent and redeem the situation. In the rule of law a penalty is one of the many consequences that may follow upon a failure to fulfil an obligation, but it is annexed to an obligation: to suffer it is not an acceptable alternative to fulfilling the obligation and it cannot (and is not designed to) restore the situation to its condition before the delinquency was committed. The fear of having to suffer a penalty may, of course, deter a potential delinquent and the expectation of a penalty may be a reason for fulfilling an obligation, but this mode of association is in terms of the recognition of obligations and penalty is extrinsic to obligation. Here a penalty is the sentence of a court of law. A law may annex a mandatory penalty to an action convicted of

[8] The oath of an English judge to render justice 'according to the law' reflects the notion of the rule of law.

breaching it, but to assign it in a particular case entails deliberation, and for a court to have some latitude in this matter, and for it to invoke prudential considerations, does not conflict with the rule of law. And although such penalties are, in general, authorized by law, to submit to them is not to subscribe to the non-instrumental conditions imposed by law upon self-chosen action and utterances; they come as the *commands* of a court addressed to assignable persons to perform substantive actions or to suffer substantive deprivations, and they invoke obedience.

There is a third condition of association in terms of the rule of law, namely, power: offices equipped with procedures composed of rules and authorized to compel the performance of the substantive actions commanded by a court of law, and custodians of 'the peace', similarly equipped, concerned to detect and to prosecute alleged illegalities and to forestall imminent breaches of the law.

7

Here, then, is a mode of human relationship, distinct from all others and, like all others, abstract: a relationship not of persons but of *personae*. Association, not in terms of doing and the enjoyment of the fruits of doing, but of procedural conditions imposed upon doing: laws. Relationship, not in terms of efficacious arrangements for promoting or procuring wished-for substantive satisfactions (individual or communal), but obligations to subscribe to non-instrumental rules: a moral relationship. Rule, not in terms of the alleged worth, 'rationality' or 'justice' of the conditions these rules prescribe, but in respect of the recognition of their authenticity.

The rule of law denotes both a strict and an unexacting relationship: here there is no place for enthusiasm. It is concerned neither with the motives nor with the intentions of actions: lawfulness cannot itself be a motive, and one cannot intend simply to act lawfully or unlawfully. It does not either demand or deny any other kind of relationship; it modally excludes all others and prescribes the conditions of a severe and an incurious kind of faithfulness or cere- moniousness which modifies without emasculating the self-chosen character of human conduct. It distinguishes between *jus* and *lex*, it recognizes a kind of moral discourse appropriate to the deliberation of *jus* and *injus*, but it is a self-sustained mode of relationship in terms of the ascer- tainable authenticity of *lex*.

This, like all other modes of human association, is a product of human imagination. But is it more than a logician's dream, a kind of geometrical theorem composed of related axioms and propositions? The rule of law may be recognized as one among the ideal modes of human relationship, but is it a possible practical engagement? Could it be made actually to occur? And further, what place, if any, does it occupy as a practical engagement in the history of human hopes, ambitions, expectations or achievements in respect of association?

On the first of these questions I do not propose to say much. Clearly, to show the possibility of *an* association in this mode requires something more than a reference to the alleged 'sociability' of human beings, their dependence upon one another for the satisfaction of their wants or their intermittent tolerance and amiability. And it calls for more than a demonstration that human beings have a strong incentive to associate in this manner. Were it to be established, an association in terms of the rule of law would certainly be a work of art. And the question is begged when it is said that all that is required to set it up is a sovereign law-making office and persons in the habit of obeying the prescriptions it issues. What we need to be shown is how the ingredients of such an association might be created and assembled; and, in particular, how human beings might acquire the condition of being *obligated* to observe the prescriptions of an *humanus legislator*.

Among theorists of association in terms of the rule of law,

Thomas Hobbes is, I think, one of the few who addressed himself exactly to this question. And he did so because his physics and metaphysics required him to display the character of such an association in terms of its 'cause' and to interpret 'cause' as how in fact an example of this mode of association might be 'erected'. The rule of law requires a known and authentic legislator. And appropriately at the centre of his attention is how to set up a law-making office endowed with authority to create obligations; and how to do this while recognizing the three fundamental principles of moral obligation, namely, that no natural man can have the authority to impose obligations on another, that no man may choose his own obligations, and that no man can become obligated save by a choice of his own. He made the problem as difficult as possible by assuming persons devoid of obligations. And he solved it by means of a neat hypothetical device (a voluntary transaction between would-be associates) for which he claims no more than that it is among the possible ways in which such an association might be set up. But this is less significant than his insistence that the rule of law stands for a moral (not a prudential) relationship; that what it determines is not actions but 'the measure of the good and evil of actions'; that it may be established by the exercise of educated human intelligence, although it may need 'the help of a very able architect'; and that in order to survive it requires the continuous fidelity of the associates but not the uninterrupted observation of their obligations.

Of course, the notion of setting up such an association *ex nihilo*, like inventing a game, is absurd. One may think of many more probable ways in which the legislative office might emerge and *acquire* authority than the very difficult notion that it should be endowed with it in a constitutive act. And there are identifiable human circumstances that would stand in the way of the emergence of such an association. Like any other it is vulnerable; and, although an exact example is to seek (except perhaps the limited example provided by a game), it cannot be pronounced a practical impossibility.

The second question is historical. It concerns the fortunes and the circumstantial inadequacies of the notion of the rule of law when related to associations identified as states, particularly those of modern Europe. Here we have to do with a slender (but persistent) strand of political reflection and invention: not that concerned with the constitution of the government of a state but with its function in respect of the associates ruled; not with the actual terms in which a government might claim or be acknowledged to have authority, but with the activity of ruling. What place has the notion of the rule of law occupied in the hopes and expectations of the creators of the states of modern Europe?

As the states of modern Europe emerged from medieval realms and principalities, from the break-up of empires, from imperial fiefs or in the agglomeration of thitherto separate communities, each had laws or set about collecting a 'law of the land' from the miscellany of laws it had embraced. It was a protracted engagement. Each state came to claim the exclusive custody of its law, each had courts in which it was dispensed and some recognized procedure for making or recording new law. Some of these laws were more like regulations concerned with particular situations or occasions, but many had graduated to the condition of definitions of status and specifications of general obliga- tions or permissions and were not unrecognizable as non-instrumental rules prescribing conditions to be observed in performing self-chosen actions. And further, there was a lively tradition, deriving from ancient Rome and already for some centuries explored by theologians and jurists which centred upon the notion of the rule of law. Of course there was much else to be observed: the relics of earlier tribal forms of association, the accumulation of an apparatus of power and the construction of an efficient administrative machine, engagement in adven- tures and the collection of the means to pursue them and the inconclusive encounters of interest in which Christendom was transformed into a still to be imagined and invented modern Europe. But there was enough at least to intimate to some that a modern European state might be made to become, might need to become and might even be on its way to becoming something like an association in terms of the rule of law.

For many whose thoughts took them in this direction, the rule of law meant little more than that to rule 'signified, not an inheritance, nor a property, nor a usufruct'[9] but an office, and the design to remove from that office its surviving discretionary, prerogative, proprietory, patronal, benefactory, managerial engagements and to recognize it as a sovereign authority, the custodian of *lex* and of the judicial procedures in which *lex* was related to contingent situations. Legislation itself was a rare and minor undertaking. This, for example, was the theme of Samuel Rutherford's *Lex, Rex: the Law and the Prince* (1644). For some it entailed a reconstitution of the office designed to extinguish the dynastic and other ambitions of rulers.[10] For others (so-called *politiques*) it appeared to be the only escape from the endemic civil and ecclesiastical strife – a government not itself concerned to promote any of the conflicting interests and thus morally equipped to disarm (but not to extinguish) the contestants. Some states began by being such miscellaneous collections of diverse persons and communities that it seemed that all they *could* come to have in common was a law. And support for this view of the character of a state was found in apt quotations from ancient writers: Livy, Cicero and even Aristotle.

But any such conception of the office of rule in a state was ranged against the survival of 'lordship' and the reluctance of governments (however refurbished their constitutions)

[9] *Vindiciae contra Tyrannos.*

[10] Etienne de la Boétie connected the rule of law with a 'republic'. But much later Montesquieu considered *la loi*, properly speaking, to be characteristic only of what he called *le gouvernement monarchique* and denied it to *l'état républicain*.

to surrender any of the managerial powers their predecessors had enjoyed; and it hardly recognized the ramshackle character of these emergent states. Moreover, it had continuously to contend with sometimes carefully considered but often fanatical and shortlived engagements to create sovereign communities of 'believers' or to impose upon a state the character of a 'religious' association ruled by charismatic 'overseers' claiming, not to be the custodians of a man-made law capable of being changed, but to have access to an alleged universal 'Law of God' or to have the 'Virtue' (and so the 'right') alleged to be appropriate to direct in detail the conduct of those they governed. And, of course, to those accustomed to tribal conditions of life association in terms of the rule of law could not be anything but an ordeal, the difficult surrender of one *persona* for another.

But the most serious opponent of the emergence of anything like a state as an association in terms of the rule of law has been a strong and versatile strand in the political thought of modern Europe, the chief version of which may be called the Baconian or technological conception of a state.[11] Here, a state is understood as an association of enterprising *personae* joined in the pursuit of a common substantive purpose, the exploitation of the natural resources of its territory (and of resources elsewhere which might be acquired by settlement, force or stealth) for the well-being of the associates; the office of its government (a technocracy) as the 'enlightened' custodian and director of this enterprise; and its 'laws' as the authorization of practices and as instruments for determining priorities and perhaps for distributing the product of the enterprise: in short, what was later identified as a *Leistungstaat* or more generally as a *Politzeistaat*. This is a benign conception of a state as a rationally regulated co-operative engagement, perhaps a *solidarité commune* of some sort, not devoid of law, but ruled by a sumptuary policy devised and enforced by administrators, agencies and regulatory commissions. It

[11] Francis Bacon, *The New Atlantis*.

was later represented as an 'historical development' unavoidable in the circumstances of modern life and even as the *ur*-form of human association dialectically redeemed. Some writers have remarked upon the self-defeat inherent in this version of the quest for 'prosperity' and have' even suggested that the virtue of a state in terms of the rule of law is its superiority in this respect. But for us, here, this is of no account: what is important is its comprehensive and designed denial of the notion of a state as an association in terms of the rule of law.

And there is, perhaps, one other circumstance worth mentioning in this connection, namely, the manner in which an almost universal convention of modern politics has, as it has turned out, hindered rather than advanced the emergence of states as associations in terms of the rule of law. Political 'parties' have rarely escaped the character of organizations of interests, not necessarily the interests of their electoral supporters but interests of some sort which they regard themselves as committed to promote if they are returned to office. And, of course, this runs counter to the rule of law which is not concerned either to promote or to obstruct the pursuit of interests. That resignation of its own character which is required of a party if it is to acquire the *persona* of a legislator is, to say the least, an unlikely occurrence. Moreover, this discrepancy between 'party government' and the rule of law is not modified where a party claims to be the custodian of the interests of the majority of associates or even of the common interest of all; the more substantial such a claim is the more remote is an association thus governed from the rule of law. The virtue of 'party politics', as it has appeared in modern Europe, is to have qualified the management of a *Politzeistaat* by making it a temporary and competitive office, but it has done nothing whatever to promote the rule of law. Of course, Edmund Burke and others have had a different conception of a 'political party' in which it was not an organization of interests, common or selective, but it never caught on.

A state recognized as an association ruled exclusively by law was, then, neither new in general idea nor unheard of in somewhat qualified practice in early modern Europe; nor was it without seductive alternatives, both relics of the past and designs for further exploration. But this conception of a state has suffered from two considerable defects. First, although it has never lacked some clear-headed and appropriately exact exponents, its character has often been profoundly misconceived. And secondly, too much has often been claimed for it: when properly understood the rule of law *cannot*, without qualification, characterize a modern European state.

In the writings of many of its early exponents and for a large part of its history, a state ruled exclusively by law has been represented as a state ruled by *jus*; not merely the *jus* inherent in *lex* (which nevertheless received appropriate recognition), but *jus* in the extended sense of a 'natural', 'rational' or 'higher' law, recognized and declared (but not made) in legislative utterances and correspondence (or absence of conflict) with which endows them with the quality of *jus*. In these writings a state as an association ruled exclusively by law appears as a state not only emancipated (in terms of *lex*) from both arbitrary and managerial rule, but also from *injus* in virtue of the authenticity of *lex* (and therefore the obligation to observe its prescriptions) being determined by its conformity with *jus*. In such a state *lex injusta non est lex*. This, which historically may be called the neoplatonic view of the matter, is what meets us in Samuel Rutherford: the *lex* which is *Rex* is an indubitably just 'Law of God' which reflected in legislative declarations gives them their authority. This is what Montesquieu thought the rule of law to be. And this, in a variety of idioms, is the character of a state in terms of the rule of law which appears in the writings of numerous eighteenth-century jurists and especially the early exponents of the *Rechtsstaat*: not a *Leistungstaat* or a *Politzeistaat*, nor a *Beamtenstaat*, and not yet a *Kulturstaat* (the Germans always had a word for it), but a state ruled by *lex*, the authority of which lies in its *jus*. It was something less than the promise of the fulfilment of the dream of being, at last, ruled by incontestable 'justice', and something more than the mere extrapolation of a current tendency.

As a conception of the character of a state or of what it might be made to become, it presented some difficulties. How, for example, to identify and enlist legislators whose voice might be depended upon to be the voice of *jus*? This was a problem to which Rousseau addressed himself and not surprisingly failed to solve. Or, more radically, how to recognize the quality of *jus* when it appeared? Here, dissatisfied with the ambiguity of terms such as 'natural' and 'rational', and in order to remove *jus* from the realm of opinion and to fend off the threat of anarchy contained in the claim that the voice of 'conscience' was the voice of *jus*, the necessity of having *jus* formulated in terms of some readily available principles was early recognized. It was, indeed available in embryo in medieval intellectual tradition. And in place of a somewhat speculative 'natural law' the *jus* required to authenticate *lex* was said to reside in a set of absolute 'values', a declaration of inalienable 'rights', a charter of unconditional 'liberties', or a Bill of Rights representing a Basic or Fundamental Law.[12] And some such formulation of the principles of justice, insulated from change, was said to be integral to a state understood in terms of the rule of law and was part of the apparatus of a state purporting to be a *Rechtsstaat*.[13]

[12] Some English writers in the seventeenth century attributed to Magna Carta or to an imaginary Ancient Constitution the character of a Fundamental Law.

[13] I have excluded from this account the reflections of some recent writers (e.g. John Rawls and Bruce Ackerman) because, although they present a state as an association ruled by *jus*, they identify *jus* as a consideration of 'fairness' in the distribution of scarce resources, and 'fairness' as what rational competitors, in certain ideal circumstances, must agree is an equitable distribution. Here, *lex*, if it exists at all, is composed of regulations understood in terms of the consequences of their operation and as guides to the achievement of a substantive state of affairs.

However, the vision of a state as an association ruled exclusively by law early received an imperfect but less shaky formulation: that to be found in the writings of Thomas Hobbes. Such a state, he contended, is composed of *personae* related solely in terms of obligations to observe in all their self-chosen conduct certain non-instrumental (that is moral or procedural) conditions prescribed by a sovereign legislative office expressly authorized to deliberate, make and issue such prescriptions which constitute the *lex* of the association. Having been 'erected' and exclusively endowed with this authority, this office is protected, as far as may be, from indulging in extraneous engagements such as the management of the activities of the associates, interference with their personal beliefs, the patronage of interests or the promotion of a 'common good' other than that constituted in their observance of their legal obligations. It has no property or resources of its own but is sustained by an annual income (the proceeds of a tax on consumption) drawn from the resources of the associates and used to defray the cost of its authorized engagement. And its 'power' to enforce subscription to the obligations imposed by *lex* lies, in the end, in the disposition of enough of the associates at any one time to observe them, itself no doubt supported by any appreciation they may have of the long-term value to them in their enterprising engagements of this legal order. This power is used to punish delinquency and to deter potential delinquents, but it has nothing to do with their obligation to observe the conditions of *lex*, which lies solely in the recognition of the authenticity of *lex* as the creation of this legislative office. And if it is suggested that the expressions *jus* and *injus* are not meaningless, that even if they are not the terms of the associates' obligations they must have some significance in respect of *lex*, Hobbes's answer is brisk and decisive: authentic *lex* cannot be *injus*. This does not mean that the legislative office is magically insulated from making 'unjust' law. It means that this office is designed and authorized to make genuine law, that it is protected against indulging in any other activity and that in a state ruled by

law the only 'justice' is that which is inherent in the
character of *lex*. And, in spite of some nods in other
directions, Hobbes consistently adheres to this view of the
matter.

There is said to be a 'fundamental law' (although the
expression puzzles Hobbes), and it looks like an extrinsic
standard by which to determine the *jus* of *lex*. However, it
turns out not to be the entrenched Basic Law of a *Rechtsstaat*
but merely the proscription of conduct designed to dissolve
the entire association in a comprehensive denial of the
authority of the office of rule or the destruction of this
office: a law against 'treason' and *laesa majestas*. And there
are said to be 'civil rights' or 'liberties'. But these turn out
not to signify conduct and considerations which *lex* should,
in justice, recognize and protect; they represent conduct in
respect of which *lex* has not in fact prescribed conditions:
the circumstantial silence of the law which may at any time
properly be broken. But further, there are said to be two
kinds of 'natural law', which again suggests standards of
extrinsic justice to which *lex* should conform. There is the
'natural law' which endows every man with the 'natural
right' to do whatever may lie in his power to satisfy his
wants. But this turns out to be a 'law' of a different kind, a
sociological or a psychological 'law'. And so far from being
a model of 'justice' to be followed by a maker of *lex*, it is
precisely the unconditional state of affairs which *lex* is
expressly designed to bring to an end by prescribing
obligatory conditions upon its enjoyment. And there is the
'natural law' which purports to be a set of some twenty
prescriptions, summed up in the precept *Do not to another,
which thou wouldest not have done to thyself*, which are said to
obligate every man *in fore interno*, but in his actual conduct
only when they are declared in the *lex* of a state. But first,
this *lex naturalis* turns out not to be composed of genuine
laws capable of imposing obligations (even *in fore interno*);[14]

---

[14] Hobbes makes the proviso that only when this *lex naturalis* is
recognized to be the 'law of God' (an assumption which, like

it is composed of maxims that indicate the necessary causal conditions of peaceful association. And secondly, on inspection it transpires that these maxims of rational conduct are not independent principles which, if followed by legislators, would endow their laws with a quality of 'justice'; they are no more than an analytic break-down of the intrinsic character of law, what I have called the *jus* inherent in genuine law which distinguishes it from a command addressed to an assignable agent or a managerial instruction concerned with the promotion of interests. Thus, in spite of these intellectual excursions conducted in the vocabulary of 'natural law', the only 'justice' the rule of law can accommodate is faithfulness to the formal principles inherent in the character of *lex*: non-instrumentality, indifference to persons and interests, the exclusion of *prive-lege* and outlawry, and so on.

But if, like his neoplatonist opponents, but by another route and in another idiom, a 'nominalist' Hobbes has identified the rule of *lex* with the rule of *jus*, there is something lacking from his account of a state as an association in terms of the rule of law. He is, I think, correct in refusing to identify the *jus* of the conditions imposed upon conduct in enacted law with their relation to a supposed universal inherently just Natural Law or a set of fundamental Values, or with an enacted Basic Law or Bill of Rights said to reflect these fundamental values and later associated with a *Rechtsstaat*. The rule of law has no need of

---

Suarez and Grotius, he acknowledges to be possible but not necessary for the rule of law) do these maxims acquire the character of law and become obligatory *in fore interno*. The stipulation that these maxims may be recognized as genuine laws imposing obligations only when they are recognized to be 'delivered in the word of God' derives from the principle that a precept cannot be a genuine law unless it has a responsible author and unless its author is known. In this sense neither 'Nature' nor 'reason' are known responsible authors, and therefore their pronouncements cannot be authenticated.

any such beliefs or institutions; indeed, more often than not they are the occasion of profitless dispute, and when invoked as the conditions of the obligation to observe the conditions prescribed by *lex* they positively pervert the association: they are the recipe for anarchy. Nevertheless, the *jus* of *lex* cannot be identified simply with its faithfulness to the formal character of law. To deliberate the *jus* of *lex* is to invoke a particular kind of moral consideration: neither an absurd belief in moral absolutes (the 'right' to speak, to be informed, to procreate and so on) which should be recognized in law, nor the distinction between the rightness and wrongness of actions in terms of the motives in which they are performed, but the negative and limited consideration that the prescriptions of the law should not conflict with a prevailing educated moral sensibility capable of distinguishing between the conditions of 'virtue', the conditions of moral association ('good conduct'), and those which are of such a kind that they should be imposed by law ('justice').

In order to be consistent, the vision of a state in terms of the rule of law should, then, be that of an association of *personae* indistinguishably and exclusively related in respect of the obligation to subscribe adequately to the non-instrumental conditions which authentic law imposes upon their self-chosen conduct; where these conditions (should they on any occasion be alleged not to have been observed) are related to circumstantial conduct in the casuistical deliberations of a court of law whose commands to perform substantive actions or to submit to substantive penalties are implemented by an expressly authorized apparatus of power; and where the *jus* of these conditions is recognized as a combination of their absolute faithfulness to the formal character of law and to their moral–legal acceptability, itself a reflection of the moral–legal self-understanding of the associates which (even when it is distinguished from whatever moral idiocies there may be about) cannot be expected to be without ambiguity or internal tension – a moral imagination more stable in its style of deliberation than in its conclusions.

Many writers who have undertaken to *recommend* this vision of a state have sought its virtue in what they present as a consequence, something valuable which may be enjoyed as the outcome of this mode of association. And some have suggested that its virtue is to be instrumental to the achievement of 'prosperity' understood as the maximum continuous satisfaction of the wants of the associates. But the more discerning apologists (recognizing the inconsistency of attributing the virtue of a non-instrumental mode of association to its propensity to produce, promote or even encourage a substantive condition of things) have suggested that its virtue is to promote a certain kind of 'freedom'. But this is misleading. These rules certainly do not themselves prescribe purposes to be pursued or actions to be performed. They do not concern the motives of conduct, and this mode of association is in terms of the recognition of obligations, not their uninterrupted observance; and all this may be said to denote a certain kind of 'freedom' which excludes only the freedom to choose one's obligations. But this 'freedom' does not follow as a consequence of this mode of association; it is inherent in its character. And this is the case also with other common suggestions: that the virtue of this mode of association is its consequential 'peace' (Hobbes) or 'order'. A certain kind of 'peace' and 'order' may, perhaps, be said to characterize this mode of association, but not as consequences.

This vision of the character of a modern European state is deeply rooted in our civilization. It was superbly pioneered, in modern times, by Bodin and by Hobbes. In spite of some unnecessary nods in other directions, its character and presuppositions were fully explored in the writings of Hegel who also rejected the notion of a 'natural law' as the standard by which *der Gerechtigkeit* of *das Gesetz* might be determined, and identified it as a

Kulturstaat. It appears in a slimmed-down version in the writings of the jurist Georg Jellinek. It hovers over the reflections of many so-called 'positivist' modern jurists. It has always had strong competitors. But it may be said to represent an enduring (though often confused) disposition of modern European inventive political imagination.

Nevertheless, although in some states the invitation to become genuine *Politzeistaaten* has been resisted, and the disposition at least to seek to become associations in terms of the rule of law has been lively, the circumstances of modern Europe have always made it impossible for any state (except, perhaps, Andorra) to achieve this condition without qualification or interruption. And I take this to be, not a criticism of the notion of the rule of law, but a warning to be exact about it and to distinguish between unavoidable qualification and corruption or vacillation.

In general, the character of a state as an association in terms of the rule of law is qualified when upon the authority and the engagement to deliberate and to make law is superimposed the authority and the engagement to deliberate and to make 'policy', and upon the authority and engagement to adjudicate is superimposed that of pursuing and administering a 'policy'. And by 'policy' I mean designs to promote and to seek to provide substantive conditions of things recognized as the satisfaction of an *interest* or held to be in the common *interest* of the associates, and which (unavoidably) subvent part of the resources of the members of the association in order to do so. To pursue 'policy' and to exercise authority to make such subventions imposes upon the associates the *persona* of members of a co-operative undertaking, upon a state the character of an enterprise association and upon government the character of estate management.

Some such common substantive satisfactions may be supplied as a by-product of the operation of the legal conditions imposed upon the self-chosen conduct of the associates: for example, the maintenance of a stable currency or the prevention of industrial or commercial monopolies, both of which (in simpler conditions than ours) Hobbes considered to be among the proper objects of government in terms of the rule of law. Here, the rule of law remains uncompromised.[15] And it is clear that, where in a state there was a strong disposition to be an association in terms of the rule of law, some care was taken not to compromise this character when statutory local authorities were set up to supply some common substantive services paid for by a subvention on local resources called a 'rate'.[16] But there has been one unavoidable contingent circumstance of modern Europe for which the rule of law cannot itself provide, namely, the care for the interests of a state in relation to other states, the protection of these interests in defensive war or in attempts to recover notional *irredenta*, and the pursuit of larger ambitions to extend its jurisdiction. And this is not on account of the complete absence of rules (although most of so-called international law is composed of instrumental rules for the accommodation of divergent interests), but because 'policy' here, as elsewhere, entails a command over the resources of the members of a state categorially different from that required to maintain the apparatus of the rule of law, and may even entail the complete mobilization of all those resources.[17]

[15] Cf. Henry C. Simons, *Economic Policy for a Free Society*.

[16] A 'rate' is a sum of money devoted to the provision of a number of exactly specified substantive benefits, and before our present confusion overtook us everybody knew the difference between a 'rate' and a 'tax'. The same confusion is reflected in the bastard expression 'local government': when 'government' is identified with the provision of substantive satisfactions the rule of law is compromised.

[17] Montesquieu conceived the governance of a State to be vested in three offices: legislative, adjudicative and an office concerned with making and conducting 'policy', particularly an unavoidable foreign policy. And he insisted that these offices should be 'separate', not merely because otherwise *liberté* would be prejudiced, but because he recognized these three *engagements* to be categorially distinct (*De L'Esprit des Lois*, XI, vi).

This, of course, does not necessarily entail the destruction of all law, but it does entail the desuetude for the time being of a state as an association exclusively in terms of the rule of law. So far from its being the case (as Hegel suggested) that the character of an association in terms of the rule of law is most fully expressed when it is engrossed in the pursuit of policy or when it is at war, these are the occasions when it is least itself. And although, even in these circumstances, the rule of law may (as Hobbes thought) be formally rescued by invoking such legal doctrines as that of the 'eminent domain' of a government to be exercised *ex justa causa*, this is only another way of saying that necessity knows no law. The rule of law bakes no bread, it is unable to distribute loaves or fishes (it has none), and it cannot protect itself against external assault, but it remains the most civilized and least burdensome conception of a state yet to be devised. And we owe it, not to the theorists, but to the two peoples who, above all others, have shown a genius for ruling: the Romans and the Normans.

The Tower of Babel

nil mortalibus ardui est;
Caelum ipsum petimus stultitia.
Horace

1

A proper story is like a river; sometimes it may be traced back to a source in the hills, but what it becomes reflects the scenery through which it flows. It has a history, and its history is marked by the appearance of new incidents or new characters; its colours change; it is told in fresh idioms; it may be concentrated into a ballad or a song only to be dispersed again in more prosaic tellings.

And a proper story has another quality besides this capacity to mirror the changes of human circumstances. It is the expression of some unchanging human predicament; as a Highland lament, composed to reconcile a passionate people to a contingent misfortune, expresses all the sorrows suffered by mankind since the beginning of time.

Mine is a proper story. Its source is in the mist-hung mountains of time past; and there is nowhere in the world where some version of it has not been told. It is to be found among the stories of the Chinese, the Caldeans and the ancient Hebrews, and among the Arab and Slav peoples, and the Aztecs of Peru. It has been told in the Greek, the Latin, the Celtic, and the Teutonic languages and in the tongues of those who for millennia have moved about the islands of the Pacific ocean. It is concerned with earth and heaven; with men and Gods and how they stand to one another. It is concerned with the conduct and the relations of human beings; and with perfection and imperfection.

The fortunes of Faust and the adventures of Don Juan are somewhat banal versions of it in which gold and girls are the centre of attention. And it is embedded in the tragic drama we know as the Arthurian legend. There (if you remember), what destroyed his Fellowship of the Knights was nothing so contingent as the infidelities of Lancelot and Guenevere. Arthur brushed these off, as did Charlemagne in a similar situation, which, appropriately enough, concerned the antics of an ancestor of Metternich. No; it was the quest of Sangrael itself, a prize that was not only a holy relic but (alas) also a vulgar cornucopia, that was their undoing. But the story is most familiar to us in the version first heard by the ancient Hebrew people, elaborated by Josephus and by the learned authors of the Talmud, and exciting the imagination of some of the early Christian Fathers. There it is the story of the Tower of Babel, and it runs after this fashion.

2

The lapsed human race released on earth was soon in trouble. Instead of enjoying one another (like poetic children) in a life of perpetual wonder at the marvels of the world, sustained by berries, or exerting themselves joyfully to discover and to cultivate the riches of the earth, grateful for what they could win from it, mankind was filled with limitless wants and with a savage urge to satisfy them. Careless of its beauty, contemptuous of its gifts and persuaded of its hostility, they laid waste the world, seeking only to gratify their perverse and insatiable desires. And their relations with their fellows followed the same pattern: they were animated by greed, envy, fear and violence.

In response to this situation, Zeus had commissioned Hermes to teach mankind how to manage the condition of mortality with understanding: the cunning of Prometheus had already enabled them to exploit the resources of the earth, but they had yet to learn how to accept *rerum mortalia* with grace. But the God of Israel, a somewhat different character, was so appalled by their depravity that he even repented of ever having 'made man upon earth' and was determined to start afresh. His design was 'to bring a flood of waters upon the earth', to destroy all living things save exemplary representatives of his creation, and to regenerate the human race from the one family which, on account of its virtue, should be rescued from the deluge: namely, that of the widower Noah, his three sons Shem, Ham and Japhet and their wives.

Noah and his family, by the grace of God, survived the flood that inundated the earth. 'The windows of heaven were stopped, the rain from heaven was restrained', the earth became dry land once more, and God set a rainbow in the sky as a sign that he would never again deal so drastically with human depravity; and, indeed, would in future protect mankind from the worst natural calamities: a sign that was later to be confirmed in a covenant with Abraham. Thus God, Nature and Man were reconciled each to each in a promise, not of love, but of decency and forbearance. Noah lived 350 years after the flood, quietly cultivating his vineyard and enjoying the restoration of changefulness to the world – of seedtime and harvest, of summer and winter, day and night, sunshine and rain.

On his death, Shem became the head of the family. He was a simple man, and became for later generations the emblem of a human race at truce with the forces of Nature and anxious to obey the commands of God – a rather dull race genuinely grateful for being alive, but without either nostalgia for the lost Garden of Eden or paradisical expectations; a race which, if it kept to its pious resolve to observe its side of the covenant, would give God no trouble, but (as St Augustine later conjectured) might very well cause him to yawn with boredom.

Japhet's fortunes are no part of this story; and this is perhaps not insignificant. For the land of Japhet is Europe whose inhabitants, although they are not at all immune to relapse into antedeluvian depravity, have reconciled themselves to their expulsion from the Garden and have come to regard their eternal salvation as God's business, not theirs: the inventors of civil intercourse, a somewhat precarious peace among themselves which, so far from 'passing all understanding', was very well understood by both Hobbes and Hegel, though not easy to sustain.

But Ham, unlike his brothers, was an *esprit fort*. In earlier days he had earned his father's displeasure on account of several disreputable escapades. He had married young, and was reputed to have made love with his wife while on board the Ark, which, in the circumstances, Noah considered to be irresponsible conduct. Further, during the voyage (if it may be called that), when things were naturally somewhat disordered, he had stolen a family heirloom, namely, the garment which God had given to Adam on his expulsion from Eden, and with which our common ancestor replaced his first extemporized covering. And later, by chance rather than design, Ham had been amused to see the nakedness of his father when Noah lay drunk and uncovered in his tent. The other two sons had the decency to avert their eyes on that occasion. In short, Ham was the black sheep of the family in, as it happens, more than one sense of the expression. These, no doubt, were merely personal delinquencies, revealing only a mildly impious, or even just an adventurous, disposition. But Ham became a man of masterful ambition and energy, up and doing while Shem was on his knees; and he displaced his elder brother as manager of the family fortunes.

Ham begat Cush, and Cush begat Nimrod who is the

central character in the story. Nimrod was the spoilt child of his father's old age. He grew up something of a delinquent. He played truant from school, he became a gang leader at an early age, he was always larking around with the girls, he paid little attention to his prayers and was openly disrespectful to Abraham (the son of Shem) who by then was the titular head of the family. Perhaps Nimrod as a teenager may be discerned as the first of the Hell's Angels – noisy and disruptive.

When Nimrod came of age his father gave him the garment which his disreputable grandfather Ham had stolen from Noah's baggage in the Ark. This was, perhaps, the height of paternal folly. The story is silent about the shape and colour of this garment, but it was generally believed to have magic qualities. According to legend it had been made to God's order by Enoch, the first tailor in the history of the world. On Adam's death it had been returned to Enoch who then gave it to Methuselah; Methuselah bequeathed it to Noah who took it with him into the Ark. Vested in this garment, Nimrod not only felt himself to be a fine fellow, but believed himself to be invincible. Thus Nimrod, the inheritor of the *libertin* disposition of his grandfather Ham, the spoilt son of his doting father Cush, became recognized as a notable adventurer; without deference to his elders, a law unto himself and well endowed with the charisma of impiety. He was admired for his audacity and he acquired a considerable following of flatterers and hangers-on who, dazzled by his blasphemies, surrendered to his leadership.

But he was uneasy. In spite of feeling himself to be invincible he feared that another, mightier than he, would appear and destroy him. Moreover, although he was apt to dismiss the legends of his people as old wives' tales invented to frighten children, he was aware that there was believed to be a God in heaven who might cause his downfall. Indeed, he knew at least by hearsay that years ago this God had not hesitated to inundate the earth on account of the depravity of its inhabitants, and he was disposed to disbelieve the story that this would never happen again.

Nimrod was nervous beneath his bravado. His was the classic predicament of the *libertin*, so brilliantly imagined (indeed experienced) by Pascal. He could not quite bring himself to announce that 'God is dead', or even that God was discredited and now out of harm's way, hiding in Peru. But being a man of energy he was determined to deal radically with an insecurity that had become an obsession. It was no good trying to outwit or to intimidate God, or to rely upon the possibility of his demise: he must be destroyed.

To this end Nimrod called together his followers who by this time were considerable in numbers but not in intelligence. He addressed them as follows.

> We are surrounded by enemies and the most threatening of these is this God with whom Abraham is in league. Come; let us go out into the countryside and build a city where we may do as we please with impunity. And let us call this city the city of Babel: the city of Freedom. And so that we may never again be destroyed by a deluge from heaven, let us build a tower so lofty that it will out-top any flood, so strong it will resist any earthquake, so incombustible that lightning cannot destroy it. Let us, from the top of this Tower, build out great arms which shall prop up the heavens so that they may never fall upon us again – for, as we know, the sky is a great sheet of canvas spread out by God to keep back the waters which would otherwise inundate the earth. Indeed, when we have built this Tower, let us climb up into heaven, break it up with axes and drain away its water where it can do us no injury. Thus shall we avenge the death of our ancestors and make ourselves for ever secure from the hostility of both God and Nature.

To some of his followers the presumption of Nimrod's

proposal was somewhat alarming. But after some hesitation and looking round, they applauded it. Indeed, they
had already gone so far with him that they were hardly in a
position to turn back from anything he suggested.

The adventure was set on foot next day. A site for the city
was seized from some neighbouring shepherds, a rough
wall was thrown round it, some shacks were run up, and
without delay Nimrod and his followers set about the task
of building the Tower. It was not long before the enterprise
absorbed the whole of their attention. In the undertaking to
subjugate God and Nature to human ambitions they had
stumbled upon a life-work and had become the slaves of an
ideal.

They built with passion and with energy, careless of
everything but the achievement of what they had undertaken. If, in the course of the work, a man fell and was
killed, they took no notice. But if the bricks gave way or if
some hitch occurred, there was an outcry. Delays provoked
protests, malingerers were prodded, holidays forbidden.
None was exempt, or wished to be exempt, from this
greatest of all adventures in impiety whose architect was
Nimrod himself. All gave themselves to the task, the
younger dreaming of the security that would follow from
its accomplishment, the not-so-young half-regretful of
their destiny to spend themselves in the purchase of what
they might not live to enjoy.

Meanwhile great-uncle Abraham had observed what
was afoot in Babel and was appropriately horrified at its
impiety. He prayed to God (who, until then, had hardly
noticed what was afoot) to frustrate the builders of the
Tower. Indeed, he suggested that this could be most
conveniently achieved, not by a second deluge which
would engulf all mankind, but in a more economical
manner by 'confounding the tongues' of Nimrod and his
fellows so that no man among them could understand what
any other said when he spoke. Accordingly God commanded the seventy angels who surround his throne to
descend upon Babel and to bring this disaster upon its

inhabitants. This they did, leaving behind them a people unable to pursue any co-operative enterprise. Orders were given which were not obeyed because they were not understood; tempers became frayed; exasperation spread; and frustration reached such dimensions that the people of Babel were no longer able even to tolerate the presence of one another. Thus, not by a deluge, but in a flood of meaningless words, was the empire of Nimrod destroyed. Its gibbering people separated and spread themselves over the face of the earth. Its Tower became a crumbling memorial to an impious adventure, and the name of Babel, which had originally meant the City of Freedom, acquired its historic meaning: the City of Confusion.

There are, of course, other versions of this story. According to Muslim tellers it begins with Nimrod and his libertine fellows so exasperated with the pious preaching of Abraham that they threw him into a furnace. But when he came out unharmed they were dismayed and took it for a sign that the God of Abraham was both hostile and dangerously powerful. And Nimrod in a fit of arrogance, which went beyond anything he had hitherto perpetrated, declared that he would himself mount up into heaven and dispose of the God of Abraham before worse befell. His wise men told him that the gap between heaven and earth was very great, so Nimrod ordered his fellows to erect an immensely high Tower to bridge the distance. They laboured three years. But, although Nimrod ascended it every day hoping to be able to launch his assault upon God, the sky from the summit never seemed to get appreciably closer. Urged on by Nimrod's unreasonable demands, the builders grew careless and the Tower collapsed. Thus frustrated, Nimrod sought another way of getting at God. He had made a large wooden box and to its four corners he attached ropes which he wedged into the beaks of four gigantic birds, named Rocs. They bore him, seated in this box, high into the sky. But as he neared the gates of heaven the box was upset by a gust of wind and Nimrod fell out on to a mountain top.

Frustrated a second time, he returned to the project of building a Tower, but without much confidence. The impetuosity of the builders was once more their undoing: the Tower collapsed burying Nimrod in its ruins. And this was the end of a visionary who had degenerated into a recognizable crank, a figure of fun.

And there is a Caldean version of the story in which Nimrod appears as an early Babylonian king who, filled with folly, led his people in an assault upon heaven, only to be frustrated by a whirlwind that swept them from the earth. But the ancient Hebrews, who were tireless in their elaboration of this theme, had another and grimmer version of it. In this account, Nimrod is represented as so *farouche* a character that even his followers drew back from his impieties. Deserted by his subjects, he determined to go it alone in his assault upon God. He constructed a bow of extraordinary dimensions and unusual power and with it he shot an arrow into the sky, aimed at God. The arrow fell to earth dripping with blood. But Nimrod did not survive his triumph. He collapsed upon the ground, and as he lay, too feeble to move, a host of ants devoured him.

The theme of this story is, then, a titanic assault upon heaven. In the most ancient versions of it, heaven is the abode of a somewhat severe God who is interested only in good and evil and is indisposed to make allowances for those who, not always lacking good intent, find it difficult to avoid the ordinary negligences of a human life. And it looks back to the Flood, the occasion when God demonstrated both his impatience with human depravity and his command over the destructive forces of Nature. Thus those who rebel against such a God are a people who do not see why they should have their delinquencies taken so seriously but wish only to avoid the consequences of depravity. They seek relief from a potentate in whose promises they have no faith. The story is concerned with avoiding a real or an imaginary reign of terror, and with the achievement of absolute security from the hostile powers of God and Nature. If, like Nietzsche, they could convince themselves that this terrible God was already dead, they would (it is true) cease to feel themselves threatened. But they could be certain of the security they were seeking only if they had the assurance of his demise which belongs to a successful assassin. Nimrod is cast in this role of an heroic killer. There is no design to occupy heaven, which (in most of the versions of the tale) is no more than a reservoir of enormous proportions whose waters are held back only by a precarious God-controlled sluice; the aim is only to destroy it and its proprietor.

But even in ancient times the story of Babel was made to bear other, both deeper and more trivial, meanings. It pointed back beyond Noah and the Flood to that first, almost inadvertent, excess and the loss it entailed. It is a deformed expression of that nostalgic longing to be delivered from postlapsarian exile and to return to the Lost Garden: a loss which the record shows to have been occasioned not by a rebellious Adam but by his decent resolve to stand by his rather foolish wife who had been gulled by a slick encyclopaedia salesman into undertaking a purchase of knowledge that was beyond both their station and their means. For in some of the stories which revolve around Nimrod this dream of enjoying once more the peace and plenty of the legendary walled Garden has been transformed into a monstrous design to storm heaven itself. Nimrod is not a petty thief, like Prometheus; he is the leader of a cosmic revolution whose enterprise is not only doomed to failure but entails the destruction of all the virtues and consolations of the *vita temporalis*, a destruction of which the 'confusion of tongues' is the emblem. But, of course, the symbolic radiance of this tale does not compare with that which has been evoked from that brief encounter of God and man which constitutes the mysterious story of Cain.[1]

In later times, Dante identified Nimrod as a deformed human being, a giant, who out of vanity made war upon heaven and in consequence confounded the conversation

[1] Ruth Mellinkoff, *The Mark of Cain*.

of mankind. He is discovered in the ninth circle of the
Inferno, a gibbering idiot forever blowing a tin trumpet: *O
anima confusa*. In Ariosto's poem Nimrod appears appropriately as the ancestor of the loud-mouthed Rodomont,
the most terrible of all the Saracens, and the inheritor of
Nimrod's garment of invincibility (here depicted as a
dragon's skin), the lack of which (he had carelessly left it
hanging on Isabella's tomb) was to cause his downfall in his
final encounter with Bradament. And, of course, the
Nimrod who has come down to us is a mighty hunter, but
characteristically (in the words of Montaigne) he loved only
the prey and not the chase. More prosaically, Babel has
been read as a commonplace tale of benevolent despotism:
Nimrod is the first self-appointed Redeemer-King whose
authority rested upon the stirred-up fears and resentments
of his subjects. And Hegel, of course, goes back to the
beginning. He recognizes the Hebrew story of the Flood as
a rift between Man, God and Nature healed, only to be
reopened in the tale of Nimrod. And he contrasts this story
of Hebrew excess with the Greek story of Ducalion and
Pyrrah. There, even the unexacting Zeus is finally exasperated by the rapacity of the human race and resolves to
destroy mankind in a Flood. But Ducalion (a son of
Prometheus) and Pyrrah, man and wife, on account of their
uncommon virtue, are saved in a boat. And the regenerate
race, which Zeus allows them to beget after the Flood has
subsided, enjoys a golden age of harmony unbroken by the
vulgar ambitions of a Nimrod; a harmony which gradually
evaporated but which, before it did so, was perhaps caught
up in the legend of Diana, that undemanding girl whose
only wish, in the words of Chaucer, was

For to walken in the woodes wild.

However, borne upon the river of time, this tale of Babel
and Nimrod, as it reaches our own age, has been told in a
somewhat different idiom. The new features of the telling
have, of course, their counterparts in the earlier versions;
the change is one of emphasis. It is still detectably the same

story even if the *mis-en-scène* is different and the banalities of modernity qualify the heroism of ancient impiety.

3

In this version of the tale the curtain rises upon Babel, a city full of the bustle of getting and spending. A vast variety of enterprises is afoot; there is an endless proliferation of wants and satisfactions. The inhabitants are noted for their fickleness. The general atmosphere is one of moderate vulgarity. Art has degenerated into entertainment and the entertainments are apt to be crude. The Babelians have no spectacular vices, and no heroic virtues. They are easily seduced by novelty; if they had Madame de Sévigné's gift of introspection they too would exclaim: 'Dear God, how I love fashion.' They are self-absorbed and self-indulgent. It is indeed a City of Freedom: the home of every imaginable lib.

Yet a stranger come among them might have recognized them to be a difficult people. There is an undercurrent of discontent, an aimlessness and an absence of self-discipline. The Stoic and the martial virtues are notably absent from their character. They are a wayward rather than a listless people; and they are resentful of government, not as a wild and passionate people may be, but in the manner of spoilt children. Indeed, such order as there is among them has for so long been maintained by bribes, that this is the only kind of control they now tolerate. In short, Babel is a *civitas cupiditatis*, and its inhabitants, although not strikingly affluent, are a people devoted to affluence. From one point of view this tale of Babel is that of the nemesis of greed.

They are ruled by a young duke, Nimrod, who has recently succeeded to his father's estate and authority. In many respects he is a typical Babelian. The ducal family in which he had been brought up was a near replica of the city itself. From infancy his most casual wants have been waited upon and his most wayward demands satisfied. And the deference to his desires which he had enjoyed as a child from his parents and tutors he naturally expects to receive from his people now that he has become their duke. But since their expectations are similar to his own (namely, the ready satisfaction of all *their* wants), and since these are without limit, duke and people find themselves pulling in somewhat different directions. This difficult situation may be said to have been potential in Babel ever since the time of the first duke, Ham; but the accession of a new ruler had brought it to a head. And Nimrod, impatient of the frustration it promised, addressed himself to the resolution of the conflict.

In the events that followed it is difficult to say exactly what part was played by the duke's determination to organize the activities of his people so that they should contribute to the satisfaction of his own limitless wants, and what part sprang from the greed of the Babelians. No doubt duke and people both believed themselves to be on to a good thing, and it may even be that the duke thought that his people would become more manageable if he appeared to be entering into a benevolent alliance with them. But what is certain is that these events could not have come about were it not for some important beliefs shared alike by duke and people.

It may be said of the Babelians that, like the Borgia Pope Alexander IV, they believed to a limited extent in almost everything. But their pragmatic disposition was anchored in what, for want of a better word, may be called some religious beliefs. In these God did not appear as the ruler of the inhabitants of the earth, pleased when they were well behaved and implacable towards wickedness, but as the proprietor of an estate situated above the skies. It was an estate of unimaginable wealth, reputed to contain all that was desirable in limitless profusion. The sun shone by day and the nights were as soft as velvet, lit always by the moon at the full. It was a world without winter. The trees were always in fruit; and through it there meandered a river of wine. All that could be asked for was in instant and unlimited supply.

The proprietor of this miraculous estate was understood to be well disposed to the dwellers upon earth; indeed, he was recognized as the ultimate source of all their satisfactions and enjoyments, which (so to speak) were directly or indirectly the produce of his heavenly estate. He was known to have moods of capricious generosity when he would let down from heaven on a string a basket of figs or pomegranates from which lucky passers-by could help themselves. But he was known, also, to be of a somewhat stingy disposition, doling out enjoyments to human beings in a miserly fashion, whetting but never satisfying their appetites. In short, the earth was recognized to be a distinctly inferior part of the universe, a region of scarcity, and its inhabitants to be what the theologians called 'underprivileged'. Thus, the God of the Babelians was known as a close-fisted benefactor, the author of all their enjoyments but also of all their privations. And since, like spoilt children, they could not understand why they should ever be called upon to suffer privation, they were more resentful on account of what was withheld than grateful for what was given. These beliefs, shared by duke and people alike, were the soil in which Nimrod planted a seed that was to flower in a revolution in the Babelian way of life.

On the anniversary of his succession to the dukedom Nimrod held a durbar at which he made a long speech. He began by praising his people for the ingenuity with which they invented new wants and for their resource in satisfying them. The moderate affluence which lapped their lives was all their unaided achievement. But he was aware, also, of the privations they suffered and he went on to commiserate with them for their frustrations. He displayed himself as a man of limitless generosity but sadly restricted means. Indeed, his brains were of more use to them than his wealth. And he proceeded to show himself to be a man of large ideas.

I will not insult you [he said] by suggesting that you remedy your privations by engaging in any of the fashionable gnostic expedients, such as the manufacture of silicon chips. Nor do I suggest that you (and here he hastily corrected himself) that *we* should divert ourselves by building anything so irrelevant as a Dnieper Dam. Let us leave all that to others. Your dignity as Babelians demands a more radical recognition. For who is the real author of your frustrations? Who is it who has the means to put an end to your privations, to endow you with a limitless profusion of satisfactions, and does not do so? Is it not this miserly God who wantonly witholds what he might give with no loss to himself? Do you not deserve better than you receive? Are we not the innocent victims of a cosmic conspiracy? Or, if not this, then at least of a criminal distributive injustice?

This part of his speech Nimrod had to manage with some care because he might easily have lost the sympathy of his audience by over-balancing into manifest blasphemy. The Babelians were in many ways an unpretentious people, unaccustomed to having their dignity invoked. Moreover, ordinary men may grumble at their lot but they are slow to impugn their Gods even if they endow them with discreditable characters. Other peoples before and since have been incited to resent their exclusion from what has been called 'a place in the sun', but human discontent usually centres upon the lack of what others are seen to be enjoying and not upon totally imaginary satisfactions. But having prepared his audience for something unusual, he went on to confide in them an ambition which, he said, it was his dearest wish to achieve on behalf of his people, and the plan for its achievement which he had hatched with the aid of his faithful vizier.

The ambition was no less than that of forcing open the gates of heaven, dislodging this miserly deity from his estate and appropriating for the enjoyment of all Babelians the limitless profusion of paradise. The plan was to build a Tower far into the sky from which this assault upon heaven should be launched. The speech ended with an exordium that clothed the project in the colours of a holy and profitable war.

When Philip, the father of Alexander the Great, announced an inordinate adventure it was said that his valet was wont to caution him: 'Philip, remember that you are mortal', which, of course, meant nothing so banal as, 'Remember that you will die.' But Nimrod, on this occasion, received no such reminder. Nevertheless, there was much in the character of the Babelians that would not dispose them to engage in so extravagant an enterprise. They had always preferred to arrive rather than to travel, and they would naturally have wished others to undertake it and that they would come in at the end to enjoy the fruits. They had their share in the Faustian preference for magic, but they had always regarded Aladdin as a lucky boy who had hit the jackpot, a piece of good fortune not to be looked for in respect of a whole people. Indeed, it is impossible to imagine any people seriously entertaining such a project unless they had been incited to do so by some masterful visionary, or that their embarking upon it would entirely allay the feeling that it was too good to be true and the suspicion that it must be a hoax. But be that how it may, when the sun went down a profound change had come over the people of Babel. Some would say that greed had defeated both indolence and sense; others that they had at last found a purpose in life to contain their waywardness and had raised themselves to the status of priests of an ideal.

The Babelians, then, were not a people who might have been, even briefly, uplifted by the glorious vision of tractors rumbling into the red sunset, all grievances swallowed up in the bleary rapture of comradeship devoted to the conduct of a white-hot technical revolution, either for its own sake or for its prospect of opulence. They were capable of envy and resentment; but what joined them was a profound feeling of being alike 'deprived': allowed to have wishes but denied their immediate satisfaction. What they might seek, and now heard themselves being offered, was an 'alternative' to their circumstance at once recognizable (asking for no dispositional change in themselves) and so radical that even they could not expect it to be achieved overnight or without some effort.

4

Work on the Tower began without delay. A site of several acres in the middle of the city was cleared. And at once the consequences of the undertaking began to reveal themselves. A small part of the site was occupied by a sweet and tobacco shop, and when the bulldozers arrived to sweep it away, its elderly proprietor went to the city offices to protest and to claim compensation. He was a man of some address and brushed aside the counter girl's advice that he should submit his complaint in writing; he insisted upon seeing the clerk to the city. This official admitted that the situation was unprecedented and regretted that he had no power to stay the demolition, but he promised to bring the matter before his Council. Others damaged by the antinomian enthusiasm with which the new 'social purpose' of the Babelians was embraced resorted to the High Court; but their complaints received a dusty answer. In one celebrated judgement a distinguished Justice (named Lord Wensleydale) declared that when great works were afoot designed to increase the prosperity of all, private convenience must yield to public good. And this confirmation of the sovereignty of the *utilitas publica* terminated the civil history of Babel.

It is possible that had the inhabitants of the city been able to foresee what their engagement would entail, they might have started upon it with less enthusiasm. But, of course, these entailments only slowly revealed themselves. As at the beginning of a war the pattern of life changes but slowly, so in Babel the conditions of this undertaking to invade and capture paradise only gradually became evident. Indeed, it was something like a twelvemonth before the Babelians began at all clearly to recognize themselves to be engaged upon an enterprise that called for the total mobilization of their resources. This City of Freedom was becoming a community and its inhabitants were in the process of acquiring a new communal identity in place of their former distinct individualities. But whether the identity was that of Heaven-Seekers, or merely of Tower-Builders, remained obscure.

The first year or more was a period in which enthusiasm for the project took many different forms. The Administration of the city took the lead. New postage stamps were issued depicting a tower, rather like the castle in a chess set. And before long new coins were minted with a tower on the obverse and Nimrod with a miniature tower in his hand on the reverse. After this, the obsession began to take hold. No people, least of all the Babelians, can feel itself seriously engaged without the engagement being translated into the terms of toy-making and 'show-business'. Plastic towers took the place of plastic gnomes in suburban gardens. The design of children's toys was invaded by the tower *motif*. Transfers depicting a tower were sold for the windscreens of motor cars, and stickers with slogans such as 'Up the Tower', 'Build for the People's Paradise' and 'Take the Waiting out of Wanting', for the back windows. The gingerbread buns which the children of Babel were accustomed to take to school were baked in the shape of a tower. And items such as *Steak à la Tour* and *Consommé Touraine* appeared on the menus of restaurants. The articles of brides' *trousseaux* had a tower embroidered upon them in the appropriate places. And, of course, 'tower' both as a noun and a verb, was endowed with an obvious secondary meaning. Turita became the popular name for girls, and Tar for boys.

These frivolities, however, gradually faded from the scene. One by one occupations and engagements extraneous to the undertaking disappeared, and the activities of the Babelians began to contract around a single centre. Their proverbial gaiety gave way to a spurious kind of gravity.

The children of Babel had never enjoyed very much in the way of schooling; life began early and it was concerned with the satisfaction of wants which called for little learning. Its university was a tribute to the culture of earlier times (Babel had not begun in barbarity), but learning was sought by only a few. And there was an art school presided over by an artist of distinction who had emigrated from Paris. But under the inspiration of the new 'social purpose' all this quickly revealed itself to the planners as the makings of an 'educational system' designed to impart (as a famous report put it) 'the skills and versatilities called for by the current engagement of the people of Babel'. A new A level subject called Tower Technology (TT for short) was introduced, a degree in Tower Studies was added to the curriculum of the university, and the School of Art was converted into a School of Industrial Design. But these were no more than early adventures in a transformation that was to leave nothing unchanged.

A people consecrated to the achievement of a perpetually rising so-called 'standard of life' is only a dim reflection of the devotion of the Babelians to a total satisfaction, not in instalments, but as a final reward. Those who did not themselves work on the Tower were devoted to the care of those who did. The collection of rations came to take the place of shopping. The distinction between rich and poor ceased to exist; all alike were pauperized. And, in the end, the only remaining use for money was to make bets in the betting shops on the next day's achievement of the builders, and to win or to lose entirely notional sums. Where there was only one subject of talk, imagination and language became impoverished. Newspapers degenerated before they were replaced by thrice-daily official bulletins on the progress of the Tower, broadcast on what, oddly, became known as the media. All conduct was recognized only in its relation to the enterprise. The words 'good' and 'bad', 'justice' and 'injustice' acquired restricted meanings appropriate to the circumstances: to each was affixed the adjective 'social'. And there emerged among the Babelians an *interimsethik* to match the character and the purported evanescence of the current manner of life.

As the obsession took hold, nobody was in doubt about why he was alive. Identity crises ceased to be fashionable; 'alienation' was a word of the past; the suicide rate dropped to nil. But some new diseases made their appearance. In one, which the doctors called *melancholia turita*, the sufferers, after displaying a variety of symptoms such as 'seeing towers' or believing that they were being raped or devoured by towers, usually ended with the conviction that they themselves had been transformed into towers – a veritable *Turmerlebnis*. Indeed, besides the Tower itself, the only building projects undertaken at this time were the construction of mental hospitals and clinics to deal with the proliferating anxieties the enterprise generated.

It was only to be expected that this new 'lifestyle' as it was called should meet with some resistance. It was made fun of by satirists; it was preached against by the pious; old-fashioned parents scoffed at it when their children came home from school filled with the latest lunacy; and there was still company in which a young man who had been awarded the Tower Medal (4th class) was ashamed to show his award. But this scepticism was combated by a barrage of propaganda. The liturgies of church services were revised, and a New Theology emerged, disseminated in pamphlets written by persons who came to be known as the Tower-Side Bishops, in which the doctrine of the Miser God was propounded. Even the early history of Babel was rewritten so that the past could be accommodated to the present.

Meanwhile the work proceeded apace. The foundations had been laid with care and only after the materials had been subject to exhaustive tests. Architects with plans stood beside masons and bricklayers, and overseers supervised the placing of every stone. The Tower was visited every day by Nimrod who occasionally laid a ceremonial brick. Whatever the enormity of the enterprise, there was nothing negligent or slipshod in the manner in which it was pursued. And this care and concern extended far beyond the materials and techniques used in the construction of the Tower. Indeed, the very extravagance of the undertaking seemed to require that it should be endowed with an unusual degree of self-consciousness. What, however, it evoked was not reflection designed to accommodate the laboriousness of the undertaking to a native urge to grasp and enjoy immediate benefits, but an almost insatiable curiosity about the feelings and attitudes it generated. For example, the Tower had no sooner got off the ground, than an enquiry was begun to evaluate its scenic quality on a bipolar semantic-differential test and the results of this enquiry were, of course, quantified. And a whole industry emerged concerned with 'enquiries' about the opinions, the motives, the hopes and fears of the inhabitants of the city. Babel became a city of polls and questionnaires, conducted for the most part by schoolchildren sent out to gather this information from passers-by. The fact, for example, that 43 per cent of the girls between the ages of 16 and 18 preferred bricklayers to masons was thought to be so significant that the weekly variations of this figure were published. Thus the social purpose of the Babelians was under continuous uncritical scrutiny. Even the least enthusiastic citizen could hardly complain that the project was not being 'well researched'.

The Tower itself was a square structure, the inside of which was composed of a spiral stairway with periodic platforms and flanked by a wide continuously ascending slipway, the whole capacious enough to accommodate the movement of the engines of war to be used in the final assault upon heaven. Much thought had been given to the design of this military equipment and arsenals had been erected to produce and store it. Nobody knew what resistance the invasion would meet. God himself was conjectured to be pretty senile, needing only to be deprived of his authority, evicted from his residence and sent to live in some suitable exile. But the mood of his retainers was expected to be hostile and their resources considerable. Heaven would not fall in a skirmish, and the policy laid down was that the invaders should be prepared for every imaginable emergency. While the builders were at work on the Tower, the assault troops were undergoing intensive training.

Years went by. As the Tower grew higher the shadow it cast on the city grew longer. After the first months of enthusiasm, the tempo of the work settled to a less exciting norm, and the work itself became a professional undertaking. And in the course of time there emerged persons who transferred their obsession to the Tower itself. They wished to demolish the work that had been done in order to embark on the construction of a better designed Tower. There was, then, some danger that their purpose might be forgotten and that Babel would become a city of beavers merely responding to an acquired disposition to lay one stone upon another. Indeed, there is one version of the story that has this undramatic ending, with Babelians degenerating into a nation of idiot tower-builders.

Moreover, the adventure Nimrod had set afoot was threatened from another direction. It is fair to say that the inhabitants of Babel never had any very clear ideas about the heavenly estate they were preparing to invade, and their theologians were, for the most part, silent on this matter, preferring to dwell upon the enormities of its miserly proprietor and the justice of his projected expropriation. Thus while the Babelians had set out upon their task as a people of many wants and had thought of paradise as a place where these wants would all be instantly satisfied, their devotion to their task had changed them into a people of but a single want – to get to heaven. But as the Tower grew, study groups were formed and gathered to listen to teach-ins designed to reveal what was to be expected. It is true that these meetings became little more than competitions in imagining new wants and imagining their satisfaction, but even so they did something to defend the Babelians from the final frustration of entering paradise and finding they had no wants to satisfy.

And the somewhat fanciful proceedings of these classes for adults had their counterpart elsewhere. Young people, preparing for what they were beginning to hope was not a life of toil, controlled by what were called 'man-power budgets', but a life of fulfilment, formed fraternities – groups who would enter paradise together in the wake of the invading armies and explore its promise of profusion. They were tired of all this talk about Tower Technology, they were tired of being told about the ingenious experiments that had been set up by a farsighted Babelian to produce the perfect bricklayer in a process of psychological conditioning. They wished only to dream of the future. So it was natural for these young people, who (unlike their elders) would not totter into paradise exhausted by their exertions, to form groups of their own, sodalities for the rehearsal of the life to come – free from consideration of likelihood and unhindered by the conditions of probability. These fraternities represented what was perhaps the last remnant of light-hearted fun in the anxious circumstances of the Babelians.

But while all these preparations were being made the courage of the inhabitants of the city was severely tested. Building materials began to run short. The supply of clay for bricks was beginning to be exhausted and the quarries had been worked until they had little more to yield. In these circumstances, the Babelians, led by Nimrod himself, determined to play their last card. Beginning with the ducal palace, the buildings of the city were demolished to supply materials for the Tower, and before many months had passed Babel became a place of tents and caravans, of cave-dwellers and inhabitants of holes in the ground.

However, it was now thought that, whatever there might be to follow, the Tower would soon be finished. The summit had long since been far out of sight to spectators on the ground and it was many hours' climb for the builders to reach their place of work. There was room now for but few on the job. The numbers of the unemployed had, of course, increased, and Babel was fast becoming a city of idlers. As with a civilization that has sold itself to machines, all were sustained, but now only a privileged few had work. But the bulletins were optimistic; confidence ran high; the last remaining critics and doubters fell silent. That spring the farmers sowed no wheat in the belief that before harvest time they would be in paradise feasting upon what would have cost them no labour. The not-unmeaty bone which the Babelians had been used to gnaw with relish had been dropped into the stream of time and they were groping for its magnified reflection.

In these days, Nimrod, often accompanied by his vizier, used to mount the Tower in the morning before the sun was up and spend the whole day upon the summit, returning only when darkness fell. Sometimes he had the air of a general planning a battle upon which he must soon engage. He gazed up and around as if he were looking for footholds for his men on the smooth surface of the sky. At other times he was observed by the workmen to be sunk in thought, communing with himself, oblivious of his surroundings. He would be heard talking to himself in words they did not understand. He would seem to fall into a trance, his eyes open but seeing nothing. He was very far from being the *farouche* character of other versions of the story, ready to shoot an arrow at God should he come within range, or the endlessly optative character of his youth. Indeed, he had become a rather sad and withdrawn person, gentler than in time past, and perhaps beginning to be apprehensive of a future which now seemed close. The workmen got used to this, and beyond thinking that he might be going a bit queer in the head and hoping that this was not the case, they paid him little attention: the greed for the satisfactions of paradise had, particularly with the bricklayers, been transformed into the project of building a Tower. Sometimes when lunchtime came round and Nimrod seemed to be more than usually abstracted they would prompt him to open his packet of sandwiches, but they could not conceal from themselves that he was a changed man. And this went also for the Babelians in general. The years spent on this single, supreme project, marked by no interim satisfactions or opportunities (such as an annual harvest-home or the beginning of the fishing season) to break the monotony, had taken their toll in emotional stress. They were supported only by a distant and precarious vision of limitless loot.

Confidence in the nobility of a long and difficult enterprise may go far to sustain its pursuit, and it may even make its collapse endurable. Indeed, an illusion of nobility may suffice. But those who invest all their energies and hopes in an undertaking even tinged with depravity are bound to its success and are apt to acquire an obscure self-contempt which qualifies their faith, first in their fellows, and then in themselves. And after their long effort a vague mistrust of this kind had begun to seep into the mood of the Babelians. Emotionally exhausted and joined in a dread of failure, large numbers of them now virtually unemployed and with time for endless chatter, they began to find it difficult to believe that none would reveal his exhaustion in some fatally damaging conduct.

That such an enterprise should breed scroungers was only to be expected – Babelians had never been notably dutiful. But what now disturbed them was the suspicion that there might be some who were preparing to steal a march on their fellows when the time of fulfilment arrived, even if it were only buying an advantage from the officers whose duty it would be to marshal the final ascent into heaven. Or worse, there emerged a suspicion that they might all turn out to be dupes of a confidence trick designed for the benefit of others than themselves. Or were they, perhaps, the credulous victims of an illusion? Who was it who had said that all this talk of paradise was no more than a shot of opium to keep the masses quiet?

To the ordinary inhabitant of Babel, Nimrod was now a

shadowy figure. He was to be seen only on his daily visits to
the summit of the Tower. For years they had identified
themselves with the enterprise and with their duke, its
author. They were not disposed to doubt his wisdom or
competence, but the gossip of those who worked at the
summit caused them to reflect. What was he doing up there
all day long? To whom was he speaking when he seemed to
be speaking to himself? Was he already in communication
with the angels in heaven? And if so, what did this
portend? And sitting in the cave-like dwellings they had
come to occupy, a seed of unspecified doubt was sown in
their minds. Some, a prey to hardly formulated suspicions,
would get up early in the morning to watch the duke enter
the Tower; others would wait in the evening for his return,
relieved when he appeared and even reassured when he
wished them a civil 'good evening'.

But vague suspicions not decisively laid to rest are apt to
grow and take more precise shapes. People looked at one
another out of the corners of their eyes, ashamed to utter
what was in their minds. Heads nodded and then tongues
began to wag. At length their vague suspicions became
explicit doubts. Could it be that Nimrod, their trusted
duke, who was already holding conversations (from which
they were excluded) with the angels in heaven, was
planning to play them false? Could it be that he was making
arrangements himself to sneak into heaven, leaving them
behind? How else account for his conduct of late? And all
the native mistrust of a people whose deepest emotions
(whatever they had foregone to satisfy them) were greed
and resentment, rose up to confirm this doubt about their
leader. The suspicion, inseparable from excess, blossomed.

There was, however, little they could do to frustrate him
if, indeed, this was what Nimrod was planning. A deputa-
tion waited upon him. Ostensibly to ask for the latest
information, but really to get him talking so that he might
inadvertently divulge himself. But the result was inconclusive. All that could be done was to brief the few builders
now at the summit about their suspicions, to tell them to

keep their eyes open and to report any new untoward circumstance, and themselves to keep watch on his movements.

Things continued thus for some weeks. And then, one evening, the self-appointed watchers were at first disconcerted and then deeply disturbed when the duke did not appear at the exit of the Tower at the expected time. It was an evening in late June. Fraternities of adolescents (gathered at the foot of the Tower) were gaily rehearsing their entrance into paradise; idlers were standing at what had once been street corners. All the normal muted evening life was afoot. The doorway of the Bricklayers' Arms (left standing as a concession to vulgar habits) was crowded with drinkers enjoying the last of the beer (the breweries had been shut down). Darts players were chalking up the score. Mothers were rounding up their children for bed. In a quandary about what to do, the watchers waited at their posts. But at last they could contain their apprehension no longer. A shout and the alarm was raised. The course of recent events left nobody in doubt about what was happening and of the urgency of the situation. It was as if a trumpet had been blown.

People came running from all quarters of the city in panic fear that they were about to be deprived of what they had spent themselves to get. The slogan 'Take the Waiting out of Wanting' had bitten deep into their consciousness. There was a brief council of war: the scarcely coherent accounts of what was happening were carried away by the breeze; incitements to act were unnecessary. Although nothing had been planned or rehearsed, all knew what to do. In a moment the entrance to the Tower was filled with running men, women and children. Pounding up the stairway, led by the more agile among them, the entire population of Babel rushed on to snatch the reward of their labours from the hands of a man who they were now convinced was at this moment sneaking into paradise without them, having made a personal arrangement with its proprietor.

It is not to be thought that there were not some among

them who were a little ashamed at this wild exhibition of suspicion that might yet turn out to be unfounded. But these reassured themselves by thinking that if, when they reached the summit of the Tower, they were met by a grave and meditative duke preparing, a little later than usual, to descend for the night, they might turn their panic rush into a demonstration of confidence in him, putting smiles on their faces instead of grimaces of hostility, and pretending that they had come to honour him. But if such thoughts flashed through the minds of some, they did not impede the upward rush of the now silent crowd who had breath only for the climb.

The first massive surge spent itself. The climbers thinned out. The elderly fell back; the young went to the front. But there was none who did not keep moving as if his salvation depended on it. The Tower was now so high that the van of climbers would not reach the top until even the most dilatory of the Babelians had set foot on the bottom step of the stairway. Indeed, the leaders were not halfway up before the entire population of Babel was already inside, and the Tower itself had become like the containing banks of a river in spate. Some, made giddy by the spiralling ascent, collapsed and were trampled underfoot; others, pausing to catch their breath at one of the window slits, were crushed against the wall. And the confusion increased when the military formations who had been trained to lead the assault upon heaven arrived late (their barracks being on the outskirts of the city) and tried to overrun the disorganized mass of climbers.

The ascent narrowed as it went, and by the time those in front were reaching the summit an enormous pressure had been built up inside the Tower. It swayed as if it had been struck by a hurricane. And as the din of the oncoming crowd reached the ears of Nimrod, the floor upon which he stood trembled and the stones which the builders were engaged in fixing slipped from their places.

Then, with the infinite slowness with which the specta-tors of a distant mountain landslide see the earth beginning to move and hardly believe their eyes, the top of the Tower subsided. There was not much clatter. It was like a tired man falling asleep as he stands, first swaying a little, then bending at the knees, and finally falling upon his face with a scarcely audible sigh of relief.

But the collapse of the summit imparted itself to the Tower below. Soon the whole structure had become a raging cataract of falling stones; mangled bodies, first borne upon its surface, became submerged in its depths. The collapse went on far into the night and threw up an enormous cloud of dust. None had an opportunity to turn back; escape from the wreckage was impossible. There were no survivors (not even a crippled boy who could not keep up with the Pied Piper) left to wonder whether or not the suspicions that had brought about the disaster had been, after all, fanciful; none to consider whether the calamity was not inherent in the project. What had been designed as a stairway to paradise had become the tomb of an entire people, not perished in a confusion of tongues, but the victims of a delusion and confounded by the distrust which dogs those who engage in titanic exploits. And when the dawn came what had once been the city of Babel was a silent lunar landscape in which nothing moved.

> Round the decay
> Of that colossal wreck, boundless and bare
> The lone and level sands stretched far away.

Many centuries later, when the site of this city, long the abode of lizards and overgrown with purple asphodel, became the object of archaeological curiosity, an excavator turning over a weather-worn stone, came upon an inscription: one of those pathetic messages that sometimes greet us from the past. Evidently it had been composed and incised by a Babelian poet who had lived in the early years of the city's obsession with the bottomless abundance of paradise. It foreboded nothing; it was not a premonition of disaster, but a forlorn comment on the engagement itself.

On being deciphered it read:

> Those who in fields Elysian would dwell
> Do but extend the boundaries of hell.

Index